Leisure

Leisure

Its Rise, Fall, and Potential Rebirth

Jacob T. Snyder

Published by State University of New York Press, Albany

© 2024 State University of New York

All rights reserved

Printed in the United States of America

No part of this book may be used or reproduced in any manner whatsoever without written permission. No part of this book may be stored in a retrieval system or transmitted in any form or by any means including electronic, electrostatic, magnetic tape, mechanical, photocopying, recording, or otherwise without the prior permission in writing of the publisher.

Links to third-party websites are provided as a convenience and for informational purposes only. They do not constitute an endorsement or an approval of any of the products, services, or opinions of the organization, companies, or individuals. SUNY Press bears no responsibility for the accuracy, legality, or content of a URL, the external website, or for that of subsequent websites.

For information, contact State University of New York Press, Albany, NY
www.sunypress.edu

Library of Congress Cataloging-in-Publication Data

Name: Snyder, Jacob T., author.
Title: Leisure : Its rise, fall, and potential rebirth / Jacob T. Snyder.
Description: Albany : State University of New York Press, [2024] | Includes
    bibliographical references and index.
Identifiers: ISBN 9781438498768 (hardcover : alk. paper) | ISBN 9781438498775
    (ebook)
Further information is available at the Library of Congress.

10 9 8 7 6 5 4 3 2 1

For my parents, Mary and Michael

Contents

Acknowledgments — ix

Introduction — 1

Chapter 1   Classical Leisure as a "Way of Being" — 11

Chapter 2   Locke on the Necessity of Labor for Happiness — 29

Chapter 3   Vocation and the Radicalization of Labor — 49

Chapter 4   Rousseau's Harmless and Happy Idleness — 69

Chapter 5   Free Time — 91

Conclusion — 111

Notes — 119

Bibliography — 137

Index — 147

Acknowledgments

I received gracious support, directly and indirectly, from many in the writing of this book. It began as a paper for Arthur Melzer's course on Aristotle's *Politics*. His recommendation to develop the project was encouraging. Later, the project developed into a dissertation under the guidance of the late Steven Kautz. His advice was always valuable—and was so in both substantive and pragmatic ways. He was also a wonderful example of a scholar who could connect philosophical debates with contemporary affairs. His memory continues to challenge me to consider contemporary issues and how political philosophy can help us better reflect upon and act in response to them.

I would like to thank the anonymous reviewers of the manuscript, whose honest and thoughtful comments were crucial to an improved and sharpened version of the book. I also thank Michael Rinella at SUNY Press for his guidance throughout the process.

Previous versions of chapters were presented at meetings of the Midwest Political Science Association and the Michigan Political Science Association. I thank the discussants and other panel participants for their commentary. In addition, earlier versions of two chapters were published elsewhere. Chapter 1 is a revision of "Leisure in Aristotle's Political Thought," *Polis* 35, no. 2 (2018): 356–73. Chapter 4 is a revision of "Defending Uselessness: Rousseau's Harmless and Happy Idleness," *Political Research Quarterly* 75, no. 3 (2022): 906–17.

My students—at Michigan State University, Dalton State College, and the University of West Alabama—serve an important role in shaping my scholarship. Classroom discussion of various authors, from Plato to Wendell Berry, is a regular source of inspiration. And there is nothing quite like a room full of blank and empty stares to convince you that your line of thought is not as convincing or as interesting as you imagined.

x | Acknowledgments

This project would have been impossible—or at least much less fulfilling—without the support of Emma Slonina, as well as my family. And I had better not fail to mention my nieces, Lola and Gabby, who are the funniest people I know.

Introduction

Our relationship with work and leisure is undergoing revision. Our relationship to work and leisure has always been open to some questioning, but such questioning has grown, as we see in such discussions surrounding the "Great Resignation," "Quiet Quitting," and the "Age of Anti-Ambition." The general tendency of such discussions is to say, or assume, that we are increasingly disgruntled with work and increasingly open to leisure. Some bemoan this supposed movement, but others delight in the prospect of a future with much less work.

There are plenty of possible angles of approach to this revision, including inquiring into economic trends that might be introducing increased instability into the labor market, the capacity of technology to support greater leisure, and whether humans possess a natural right to free time. However, I propose that we[1] also directly address the role we *want* leisure to play in our lives. This is the more basic question. If we do desire leisure, we will certainly need to address economic realities, technological possibilities, and political policies. But all of that assumes an answer to the question of the *proper* place of work and leisure.

In the following, I address this more basic question of leisure's place in human happiness. In the case of the "Great Resignation," we should ask: Why have greater numbers of workers resigned their positions? Is it merely because of greater bargaining power on behalf of workers? Or, are people increasingly leaving because of growing discontent with work itself? "Quiet Quitting," the refusal to do more at work than what is required in a job description, further suggests an increased questioning of our value attachments. Quiet Quitters are discontented with their positions, so does this mean they are placing their plans and hopes in leisure instead? The same applies for the "Anti-Ambitious." If work is no longer the ground for our serious activity, then is it to leisure that we thereby turn?

1

2 | Leisure

If such discontent with work is real, it is not "idle" to ask the nature of leisure. If that is where we are turning, we should be curious about its nature, its promises, and whether we are fit for it. Thankfully, we are not completely at a loss. While we may have tended to emphasize work in liberal democracies, not all human societies and individuals have so valued work. Even if we have not spent much time experiencing leisure, or contemplating it, others have, and we should exploit these resources for our own benefit.

Methodology

The purpose of this book is to inquire into the concept of leisure, and to do so in a manner akin to that of Mary Shelley's Doctor Frankenstein (though hopefully with a slightly more sanguine result). Leisure is dead, and the book attempts to understand what would be necessary to reanimate it. As with Doctor Frankenstein, something like anatomy is necessary. The approach of the book, the "anatomy" of it, is a genealogy of the concept of leisure. I ask: What was leisure in its peak form in the classical age? In such a form, how was leisure understood to be connected to human flourishing? Then, what happened to leisure? What is the argument for work that triumphed and shaped the modern, liberal world? Also, what must be rejected, or lost, about work if leisure is to be regained? And finally, in the end, what does this tell us about what must happen for leisure to become a focal point of our lives?

The book is therefore a kind of intellectual history. However, it makes no claim to being a *complete* intellectual history but instead a *representative* one. The purpose of the history presented here is not the history for its own sake but for the sake of understanding ourselves. It operates on the suspicion that cultural self-knowledge is difficult and often requires more effort than we initially suppose. So, when we say we would like more leisure, what do we *actually* mean by that statement? Is it even a sincere wish? I do not think such wishes for leisure are completely insincere, but I find that we often do not fully understand what we are saying or know the full implications of those wishes. I understand intellectual history as a finding of ourselves through tracking and exploring the ideas that shape our values.

Intellectual history is useful in understanding ourselves, but it is also useful in considering possible futures. This is not simply because the past offers us examples of other options but for two more important reasons. First, it shows us what about ourselves we must reject in order to transform into something else, and, second, it shows us the bounds of that potential future. Many accounts of future leisure are insufficiently sober because of such a lack of intellectual and moral history. Without a reckoning with such history, we become like the romantic partner that is incapable of a healthy relationship because they are preoccupied with a past relationship. And like such a person, we are often ignorant of the effect that our past has on us. My contention is that a future of leisure must recognize the force and fullness of our attachments to labor before any future of leisure becomes possible.

And when it comes to considering what such a future might look like, if we prove capable of reanimating leisure, it will happen because of a certain historical development at the end of a confluence of technological progress, but just as importantly as the result of a particular political regime and its values. Not only do we need to reckon with our intellectual and moral heritage, but a sober assessment of leisure must also recognize what values are unlikely to be shed. I am assuming, reasonably I think, that all change, even extreme transformations, remain tied to context. A notable example of this posture toward interpreting change is Hannah Arendt's *On Revolution*. Her thesis is that the American revolution and founding did not arise out of thin air. Her contention is that the American revolution owes much to the English tradition, which partially explains its success. Rather than a complete rejection of the English tradition, it incorporated many elements. Whether the details of Arendt's account of the American founding are accurate is a separate question, but here I share Arendt's posture toward a very different question, and that posture means that we should never expect a founding, even one that is the result of a revolution, to not also incorporate elements of the previous regime. This is important not just for institutional arrangements but perhaps even more important for culture, widely understood. For that reason, we should not expect a reanimating of leisure to construct Aristotle's ideal regime, with its inegalitarianism and its rejection of modern forms of freedom. The strength of such values means they are likely to inform any future leisure.

Plan of Book

This book participates in the discussion of the potential future of leisure. One of the primary claims of the book is that we are not quite prepared

4 | Leisure

for such a future, but not for the reasons often suggested. Often cited as explanations for a lack of leisure are insufficient technological advancement, inadequate economic growth, and a lack of appropriate public policy. However, I argue that there is a much larger roadblock to leisure than each of these, and that is the structure of our *values*. We work not because automation technology is not yet ready, or just because our desire for wealth is unlimited, or because policymakers have insufficiently protected leisure, but also because we find work integral to happiness and moral development.

The argument for this explanation begins by confronting what is perhaps the most thorough conception of leisure, which is found in the political and ethical writings of Aristotle. Confronting Aristotle on the question of leisure—the subject of chapter 1—reveals the radical departure from our moral thinking that is required for leisure, at least in leisure's most thorough forms. I argue that Aristotle shows leisure to be more than the mere absence of work: it requires a fundamentally different posture toward living. If leisure is to become a larger component of our lives, we must go beyond seeing it as simply time without serious activity. Without any substantive content to leisure, there will be no great impetus to attain it.

As opposed to contemporary usage, there is certainly content to Aristotle's conception of leisure, and it represents what I call a "way of being." Rather than a freedom from work, leisure as conceived by Aristotle itself has requirements. Some of those requirements will be familiar to contemporary understandings of leisure, such as having enough material well-being. But Aristotle does not stop there and also includes moral virtue, intellectual virtue, and a political society devoted to cultivating leisure in its citizens. Aristotelian leisure is thereby best understood as an *achievement*, not as a resource used to achieve something else.

The classical form of leisure remains relevant in its demonstration of how demanding leisure is. At the same time, Aristotelian leisure may seem less relevant in other ways. Most obviously, Aristotle's ideal regime, which is organized around the cultivation of leisure for its citizens, partially accomplishes that leisure through slavery. Even if some accounts of substantive leisure are not so drastically inegalitarian as to require slavery, some form of inegalitarianism is part of nearly all understandings of leisure that go beyond the avoidance of work. The inegalitarianism of classical leisure assists us in recognizing two things. First, it reveals how far removed we are from the values associated with leisure. This leads to the second revelation, that if we are to achieve leisure, we must either radically change

Introduction | 5

our values or admit that leisure will take a radically different shape. An argument of this book is that a potential future leisure cannot simply be a return to Aristotle. We remain fiercely opposed to many of the values inherently tied to Aristotelian leisure, and inegalitarianism is only one of those points of disagreement. Instead, a future leisure must be coherent with at least some forms of liberal, democratic values.

Classical leisure, as a way of being, requires that we must also shut ourselves off from other ways of being. The life of leisure cannot also, at the same time, be a life of work. Inquiring into leisure allows us to examine the depth and nature of our attachment to work, which is the goal of chapter 2. There, I address Locke's liberal view of labor. Locke, also recognizing the incompatibility of leisure and labor, provides a representative and powerful argument for choosing labor. There is more depth to his account than is often recognized by scholars. The tendency is to emphasize, in any account of Lockean labor, its relation to the right of property. While this is certainly a crucial component of his thought, Locke makes further claims about the relationship between labor and happiness.

According to Locke, to thrive is to be a rational self-author. While this includes the material result of labor—property—it also includes the development and creation of the self more generally. And it is here that we see his rejection of leisure. According to the interpretation laid out in chapter 2, Locke not only finds the industrious to be worthy of gaining more property, he also finds the idle to be missing crucial components of a happy life. Laying bare Locke's elevation of work allows us to see why we might feel guilty when not being industrious or productive. In such moments, we feel that we are failing to live up to our potential and also that we are being irresponsible. If we have inhabited Locke's understanding of work, these reactions are coherent. If we understand thriving to be composed of constant creation of the self, which takes shapes within various forms of work, and if we see our obligations as similarly composed of work, then we *should* feel guilty at all nonutilitarian activity. Being leisured will be remarkably difficult with such values.

But we have gone still further than Locke. Modern conceptions of vocation—the topic of chapter 3—while greatly influenced by Locke and those like him, also radicalize his notions. In other words, many of us today are even more attached to work than Locke, who used labor as an allegory for all things good, and who argued that all recreation should be useful. For Locke, work is good because it is rational, which means rationality remains the higher good. Reason thereby becomes a limit to

6 | Leisure

work. As such, Locke would be able to separate better and worse forms of laboring. What later understandings of vocation do, as powerfully developed in Max Weber's writings, is eliminate rationality from the equation. Rationality is replaced by "personality," which need not be rational. While Weber's conception of vocation is ultimately secular, it shares with its religious counterpart a sense of revelation. As with religious revelation, there is no need to answer to reason, only to a feeling. In the case of vocation, that "feeling" is one of a fit with our personality.

Vocation thereby inherits the industry and the self-expression found in Locke but removes much of its bounds. It is self-development for its own sake. This is the reason for the discomfort felt at judging someone's choice of vocation. For many, the self-expression found in vocation is anchored to various kinds of paid labor. But there is no reason for it to be. Here is where I argue that vocation tends to undermine itself. It promises happiness in self-expression and development, but in its subservience to the logic of utility, its potential for creating happiness is severely diminished. Locke's demand that self-authorship include work is sensible because he also prescribes a particular form of rationality. However, once that demand for self-interested reason, what we would today call "prudence," is relaxed, it is less sensible to be tied to work. As such, I argue that vocation is failing and is so because of its own logic. If this line of thinking is correct, many would still feel the need to explore and develop the self but be increasingly frustrated at using the workplace as the ground of that exploration and development.

Strangely, it is the radicalization of the value in work that opens the door to leisure. By emphasizing self-development to such an extreme extent, its connection with rational utility becomes uncoupled. Rousseau, as explained in chapter 4, exploits this new understanding of freedom divorced from rationality. Coinciding with our radically independent nature, Rousseau's notion of freedom is as an expression of the will rather than a function of our reason. As such, freedom is the seemingly infantile "don't tell me what to do." It is a reaching back to an original freedom that precivilized humans possessed. True idleness, then, is what we incline to do, and it must be free from obligation. Obligation contradicts our natural freedom, but it also ruins enjoyment, however noble the activity done out of duty. Reaching back to that form of idleness, then, would also be to experience that original, independent joy that supposedly existed prior to the obligations inherent to society.

In order to do what we *truly* will, to become truly idle, our will must be free from corruptions such as the desire for reputation. In his

Reveries of the Solitary Walker, Rousseau becomes like his "savage," but with the developed faculties of the civilized. His developed faculties allow him to enjoy his will all the more, but he must strip himself, at the same time, of the corruptions of civilization that threaten his idleness. These corruptions are not limited to outside obligations but also include those internal desires for the trappings of society. Without this achievement, we cannot be truly idle, and our "idleness" will not be happy. We will be constantly considering tomorrow and its obligations, as well as yesterday and its troubles. True idleness is an infinite present. Thus, though an idleness built on freedom as inclination appears easy compared to Aristotle's cultured leisure, freeing the will is a similarly Herculean task. Despite its difficulty, Rousseau offers a form of leisure that better coheres with modern sensibilities than does the model proposed by Aristotle. Though certainly not universally shared, Rousseau's model is a clearer fit with contemporary understandings of equality and freedom.

The models of leisure from Aristotle and Rousseau, as well as the arguments for work and vocation, provide us with a sharp scalpel to dissect our contemporary use of free time in hobbies. This scalpel, which is the subject of chapter 5, allows us the ability to not only understand our free time in terms of what we ask of it, and why we ask those things of it, but also allows us to consider our free time's future shape. Both Aristotle and Rousseau force us to ask the purpose of our hobbies in different ways, but our hobbies suggest that our free time is not as free as it first seems. I eventually argue that though we think of our free time as a space to be free from utility, usefulness tends to mark our hobbies. First, given our attachments to work, we often require our hobbies themselves to be useful. Whether it be gardening or woodworking or whatever, we are inclined to hobbies that have useful results. The term "hobby" itself does not denote or connote much in the way of seriousness. Hobbies are not our primary activities but are there to pass the time. Our serious efforts are those directed to vocation. This means that our hobbies *cannot* be serious, as the majority of our efforts are directed elsewhere. Even if we do not see our work as a vocation, we are not creatures of infinite energy. In the very least, we need our hobbies to be restorative, and not all activities admit of being restorative.

And yet, hobbies are free in a way. Though it is important to notice the structures limiting hobbies, perfect freedom from influence is perhaps not an achievable standard. It is therefore still valuable to consider the freedom that *is* present in hobbies. The argument of chapter 5 is that hobbies reflect freedom as inclination, even if influenced and structured

8 | Leisure

by utility. If we are looking to a future of increased leisure, then, the shape and structure of hobbies offer an important clue to the possible directions of that leisure. In addition, it offers an opportunity to consider how we might improve our relationship with our free time, particularly by cultivating a taste for uselessness.

Place in Scholarship

This project contributes to scholarship by addressing leisure as a complete way of life. There has been increased scholarly attention paid to leisure in the last decade, but most of these works focus on whether there is a right to leisure within the liberal tradition. Julie Rose's book, *Free Time*, is a notable, and very good, example of that posture. This project is distinct in that it addresses *why* leisure should be desirable in the first place. A right to leisure only makes sense, from my point of view, if it is part of a thriving human life, and this book aims to address that connection between leisure and happiness.

It is also distinct from another type of contemporary argument about leisure: that it is useful. While I will discuss the tendency to make such arguments in chapter 5, and while I will address multiple lines of argument for leisure, I am largely devoting the following to a leisure that is valued for its own sake, not one valued because it is useful for something else. An excellent compendium of the reasons why leisure might be useful is Alan Lightman's *In Praise of Wasting Time*. Though he finds leisure good for other reasons, much of his short book points out that play, downtime, and rest make us more focused and creative. Such arguments are worth contending with, but I intend to emphasize a more substantial leisure that understands itself as valuable regardless of its utility.

The potential utility of leisure is related to a final type of understanding leisure, and that is the supposed need for balance. Just as in the case of wanting more leisure, I am unconvinced that we fully know what we are saying when we point to the need to balance work and leisure. And as a piece of advice, it is unhelpful. It is like telling those who struggle with attaining a healthy weight that they simply need to eat less. While it might be true in a sense, it is unmindful of the fullness of the endeavor. In the same way that moving to a healthier diet might require addressing values and social constraints, it is not enough to tell someone to "work less." This book attempts to confront the fullness of what it would mean to

Introduction | 9

work less, which must address our various moral and ethical attachments, and not just economics and political rights. Tellingly, no one says the reverse, that we need to limit our leisure and balance it with work—only that we need balance work with leisure. We understand leisure to be the remainder, not the primary form of existence. This book considers what it would be mean for the roles to be reversed, where leisure is the center, and work is the remainder.

Chapter 1

Classical Leisure as a "Way of Being"

Introduction

Classical leisure is a challenge to contemporary, liberal democratic, life. As Tocqueville observed, the democratic citizen views labor as a "necessary, natural, and respectable condition of humanity."[1] While contemporary thinkers on the subject of leisure, such as Pieper and Huizinga,[2] recognize that classical leisure does challenge some contemporary values, I argue that the extent of that challenge is greater than even they suppose. The emphasis of Pieper and Huizinga is on festivity and play in opposition to labor. However, when looking to Aristotle, the challenge of leisure appears quite different and even more thorough. Aristotle's account of leisure, according to the interpretation I defend here, is better understood as a "way of being" that transcends the dichotomy of work and play. I operationalize "way of being" as follows: a positive comportment that, in the case of leisure, requires virtues, material means, and an education. These virtues and this education are different from those required of occupation. As such, Aristotelian leisure should be viewed as a different way of life, rather than one of several possible conditions between which we can move and shift. In the name of "work-life balance," we cannot simply move between labor and Aristotelian leisure in the way we might be able to move between work and play. As such, my account differs from other prominent interpretations of Aristotelian leisure.[3] Most commentators hold it to be a simple condition, understood primarily as the absence of labor. This condition is still important to Aristotle, according to the typical interpretation, because it is a precondition to the virtues.

12 | Leisure

But this interpretation is incomplete. It is incomplete because leisure itself requires virtues and is best understood as an end of virtue rather than a means. Even further, leisure requires different virtues than those required for other ways of life.

This reading is suggested by the language itself. The Greek word we translate as leisure is *scholê*. In sharp distinction to our own understanding, which views leisure as the absence of work, the Greeks saw work (*ascholia*) as the absence of leisure. If we take the language at face value, it seems the Greeks treated leisure as primary, with work understood as the absence of leisure, as opposed to our contemporary treatment of work being primary, with leisure being the absence of work. This further suggests, I think, that there is more to the Greek understanding of leisure than the mere absence of work—it is not a simple lack of activity.[4] As to its role in Aristotle's corpus, leisure is central to both his political and ethical thinking.[5] For instance, the virtues aimed at leisure are required for his account of both the ideal regime and ideal life (1334a12–16).[6] Even further, the ideal regime is created with the express purpose of cultivating and maintaining leisure.[7] In order to make a case for Aristotelian leisure as a way of being, the argument unfolds in the following steps: first, a critical treatment of leisure understood as a precondition to the virtues; second, an explication of how material means and virtues are themselves required for leisure; and third, an account of leisure as an end in itself.

The primary contribution of this examination of classical leisure is the recognition of its radical departure from contemporary values. In the face of that departure, I do not prescribe a construction of Aristotle's ideal regime. As I will later argue, such a construction is improbable, to say the least, given Aristotle's inegalitarianism and his unconcern for liberal forms of freedom. Therefore, the precise *content* of Aristotelian leisure is unlikely to be of concern to those considering future leisure. However, what must be of concern, and what will be attached to all subsequent accounts of leisure in this book, is the idea that leisure is a way of being. The precise nature of that way of being, and who has access to it, is contestable; but *that* it is a way of being is not.

Leisure as a Precondition

The most widely understood meaning of Aristotelian leisure is as a means to attaining the virtues—whether those virtues are moral or intellectual.

Classical Leisure as a "Way of Being" | 13

Here it is best described as a *pre*condition. In this vein, consider the following passage from Marshall: "Agriculture is a form of life that among all actual occupations, comes closest probably to the ideal, since the life of fruit gathering, hunting, and fishing—because of the refractory character of actual nature—does not leave us enough time for the leisure required for the fuller life of man."[8] Leisure, understood here, is a particular form of emptiness. It is an empty vessel of time that is marked by the absence of work. Of course, leisure in this sense can remain important. As Marshall correctly notes, leisure is necessary for the "fuller life of man." It is a precondition but a particularly important one. Without it, we can neither attain nor express the virtues that mark the higher aims and purposes of human life.

We see a similar account in Destrée. For him, Aristotelian leisure is the "condition for the possibility of the exercise of those activities which implement the goods that are desired for their own sake."[9] Like Marshall, Destrée is correct to find this condition important, as it is the "fundamental principle" of Aristotle's ideal regime. However, Aristotelian leisure is depicted as limited to being a means to the higher goods, rather than itself being the end to which other means aim. It is equivalent to a kind of equipment. The ideal regime requires leisure in the same way it requires food and weapons.

This account of Aristotelian leisure certainly captures part of its meaning. Beginning with moral virtue, we learn in book 7 that farmers are to be excluded from citizenship in the ideal regime. The reason for this is a "want of leisure both with a view to the creation of virtue and with a view toward political activities" (1328b40–29a3).[10] Farmers are incapable of attaining many of the moral virtues because they seemingly have insufficient time away from their work. Moving to intellectual virtue, we see in the *Metaphysics*, for instance, that Aristotle finds the beginning of intellectual activity to correspond with the beginnings of leisure: "When all such arts had been built up, those among the kinds of knowledge directed at neither pleasure nor necessity were discovered, and first in those places where there was leisure. It is for this reason that the mathematical arts were first constructed in the neighborhood of Egypt, for there the tribe of priests was allowed to live in leisure" (*Metaphysics* 981b21–25).[11] Aristotle uses leisure in this instance as a precondition to mathematics. Relating to his claim in the *Metaphysics* that human beings naturally desire to know (980b21), it seems that leisure is the most crucial precondition to the development of nonutilitarian intellectual activity. The desire to know is

14 | Leisure

naturally part of us, but we are unable to indulge this desire fully when we are preoccupied with securing the means to other desires. We utilize practical knowledge when building tools to secure our basic needs, but it is not until we have freedom from labor that we are allowed to gain knowledge outside of those concerned with either pleasure or necessity. Thus, Aristotle seems to understand leisure, at times, as a precondition to both moral and intellectual virtue.

Yet, this is not the end of the story. It is not that the account of Aristotelian leisure as a precondition is simply incorrect. But it only captures half of the picture. Likely because of the modern conception of leisure, which tends to understand it simply as the absence of work, most commentators are blind to the other half of leisure. This other half is more than a negation of labor. It is an affirmation of a particular way of being that itself requires virtue, material means, and an education.

Leisure as a "Way of Being"

Paradoxically, leisure is both a means to achieving virtue while also being the ultimate end of those virtues (some of them at least). Coming to grips with both senses is our only way of getting to a complete picture of this crucially important Aristotelian concept. There are a number of components to describing something as a "way of being" that are not commonly included in everyday usage of "leisure." First, a way of being is a relatively durable comportment. *Scholê*, in Aristotle's corpus, is primary in its relationship with work. Contemporary usage of "leisure" assumes the opposite. As such, leisure is often treated as a diversion: it is not that for which we aim our life, but it is the remainder after our work is completed for the day or week. This gives leisure a strict temporal boundary, one that is determined by occupation.

What I intend by "way of being," meanwhile, is a durable turn, or comportment, of the soul. We should expect durable comportments to themselves have their own requirements. For instance, they likely require their own excellences and, perhaps, material means in order to support them. And this is precisely what Aristotle prescribes. If leisure were something less than a way of being, if it were merely a diversion from one's more serious endeavors, then enumerating virtues, and even organizing the ideal political regime around it, would be profoundly strange.

Finally, if leisure is a way of being, we should expect it to be closed off *from*, and closed off *to*, other ways of being. Whereas a temporal state is a condition in and out of which we can maneuver, separate ways of being assume different ends, and those ends cannot always be consistent. As Aristotle tells us, different political regimes aim at different ideas of the good. A regime aimed at success in warfare, as he sometimes accuses Sparta of being, has a different idea of the good than, say, his ideal regime aimed at leisure. The Spartans are incapable of being leisured, not because warfare takes up all of their time, but because they have a different understanding of the good. Furthermore, these different and often exclusive aims assume different virtues, as will be discussed later. With this in mind, I define "way of being" as a durable comportment of the soul toward a particular end that, as such, requires virtues of character, an education, material means, and a supportive political environment.

Though this way of defining Aristotelian leisure may seem abstracted from Aristotle's own language, "way of being" is not alien to Aristotle's thought. In fact, it is one way to describe, and is consistent with, the distinction Aristotle famously makes between *kinêsis* and *energeia*. Whereas *kinêsis* is a motion that finds its end outside of itself and ceases once its end is reached, *energeia* is always achieving its end (*Metaphysics* 1048b19–30, 1050a4–10). Aristotle uses the example of losing weight to describe *kinêsis*. The process of losing weight has not yet achieved its goal, and once it does, the losing of weight ceases. Meanwhile, an *energeia*, such as happiness, is always achieving itself. While most commentators describe leisure as a precondition for developing the virtues, I find leisure to be better described as an *energeia*, or activity whose end is always present. It is not simply a becoming on the way to something else but is a durable, continued, and complete activity. Describing leisure as a complete activity also has the advantage of signifying that it is not a lack of motion. Leisure, just like *energeia*, is not rest but has its own kind of work. What separates it from other forms of motion is that the end of its motion is not outside of itself. In plainer language, leisure is not to be understood as rest from work, or even an absence of work that allows for the development of virtue, but is an activity that implies and requires the use of excellences such as intellectual virtue. It is not the potential for virtue but the actuality and practice of many of those virtues.

Let us now consider in detail Aristotle's various depictions of leisure and assess whether "way of being" captures the concept's essence. The

16 | Leisure

most thorough treatment of leisure begins in book 7, chapter 14 of the *Politics*, which is fittingly the first chapter in Aristotle's turn toward the subject of education. In this section, Aristotle directs us through a series of divisions. The first divide is between the two parts of the soul: the part capable of reason and the part capable of obeying reason. The part of the soul that has reason is itself split; the two kinds of reason being active reason and "reason of the studying sort" (*Politics* 1333a24–26). After this analysis of the soul, Aristotle tells us that "life as a whole" is also split into a series of divisions: occupation and leisure, war and peace, and the useful and the noble (1333a31–33). In each case, both in the divisions of the soul and those of life, one of the two is to be preferred over the other. Aristotle gives us a clear rubric to making this judgment: the inferior is for the sake of the superior (1333a22–24, 33–36).

With this standard in mind, we are told that the part of the soul with reason is superior to the other, leisure is superior to occupation, peace superior to war, and the noble superior to the useful and necessary. In some sense, this is obvious. It may be clear in the abstract that peace is to be preferred over war. However, in practice, the relationship becomes murky. This is especially true in light of the context in which Aristotle couches these claims, which is an analysis of the education proper to the best regime. For, even if we all, or most of us, recognize that peace is superior to war, we nevertheless do not always *act* as if that were true, and we surely are not all educated as such. Aristotle appears to have something similar in mind when discussing the example of other Greek cities whose legislators did not direct their cities to the proper ends of politics and human life. Instead of organizing the city with the best things and the concomitant virtues in mind, they are "inclined in crude fashion toward those which are held to be useful and of a more aggrandizing sort" (1333b5–10). This passage also reveals what these "useful" rather than noble things are at the level of the city. The useful, by being aggrandizing, suggests an obsession with commerce and mastery of others. Mastery over others is a recognizable symptom of this problem, because, as Aristotle tells us, "rule over free persons is nobler and accompanied to a greater extent by virtue than ruling in the spirit of a master" (1333b26–28). The cities that prioritize war and domination necessarily express a mistaken set of priorities. The means come to be seen as the end, and there ensues a never-ending quest for greater wealth and mastery over others.

Thus, though Aristotle's claim that war is inferior to peace may be seen as a mere platitude, Aristotle's elaboration later in the chapter shows us that he is pointing to a real danger. Indeed, it is a rare political community that can be effective in securing its safety and interests without shrinking into a merely commercial and imperial society: "Most cities of this sort [those that initially aim toward peace and leisure] preserve themselves when at war, but once having acquired [imperial] rule they come to ruin; they lose their edge, like iron, when they remain at peace" (1334a5–10). On why cities "lose their edge," Aristotle explains that the "legislator has not educated them to be capable of being at leisure" (1334a10–11). This is one of our first hints that leisure is something bigger than a precondition to the moral and intellectual virtues. It itself requires an education and a number of virtues. It is not a simple state, but it is something that is accomplished.

Equipment and Virtue for Leisure

We first see leisure as itself an end in Aristotle's discussion of the quality and quantity of territory to be had in the ideal regime: "As far as its being of a certain quality, it is clear that everyone would praise the territory and is the most self-sufficient. That which bears every sort of thing is of necessity such, for self-sufficiency is having everything available and being in need of nothing. In extent and size the territory should be large enough so that the inhabitants are able to live at leisure in the fashion of free men and at the same time with moderation" (1326b27–32). Though Aristotle does not want fertile enough land that the temptation to immoderation is too great, he does want enough so that it is unnecessary to work tirelessly in order to acquire life's necessities. This demonstrates that leisure is not simply one of many forms of equipment needed for virtue, but that Aristotle also conceives of leisure as itself being the motivation for acquiring property and a particular standard of life. Though this does not, by itself, become a sufficient argument for leisure as a way of being, it does give us a peek—an indication of the possibility of something more.

More important is that virtues are themselves required for leisure, and those virtues are different from those required for other ways of life. The notion that virtue is required for leisure initially appears backward. If asked the relationship between leisure and virtue, most would say that leisure may be useful for some of the virtues—especially intellectual virtues. Indeed, most commentaries on Aristotle emphasize this point.[12] But to say that virtue is required for leisure is a bit perplexing. And yet, this is

18 | Leisure

Aristotle's claim: "Since the end appears to be the same for human beings both in common and privately, and there must necessarily be the same defining principle for the best man and the best regime, it is evident that the virtues directed to leisure should be present" (1334a12–15). Leisure is one of the ends of both the good regime and the good life, and the virtues should be directed at leisure in both cases. The conclusion immediately previous to this is that wise legislators should educate their citizens to be "capable of leisure" (1334a5–11). Many cities are successful in warfare, including to the extent of subjecting neighboring cities to their rule. These cities therefore have the virtues that are necessary for war. However, once in peace, they "lose their edge, like iron." Now, at this point, we could say that the virtues necessary for leisure are merely to the end of preservation. We can imagine a city that turns soft once its citizens have obtained the goods of imperial rule. If this were the extent of Aristotle's point, it would be unfair to say that the virtues are to the end of leisure, as it would seem the virtues are directed toward preservation. The section immediately following, however, tells us that war is for the sake of peace and occupation for the sake of leisure. Furthermore, the distinction between war and occupation is blurred, with leisure also suggested as the proper end of war (1334a5): peace and nobility themselves become subsumed within leisure. As such, the virtues required for peace and leisure are more than simply a means of preserving oneself and one's city.

Further, consider the specific virtues that Aristotle claims are "useful with a view to leisure" (1334a15–16). The virtues required are split in two: some virtues are needed indirectly, and others are needed directly. The virtues needed indirectly are those that are required for occupation. In order to be at leisure, whether at the level of the city or the individual, occupation is required. A city needs to protect itself from invasion if it is to have the security required for leisure, and at the level of the individual, endurance is needed to secure the means of leisure, as I need to "endure" the work that allows for leisure. This pair, courage and endurance, are the virtues required for the occupation that ultimately serves the later purpose of leisure.

There is another pair of virtues, moderation and justice, that is required both indirectly and directly. The moderation and justice that are exercised to secure the means of leisure, while being the same virtues, take on a different flavor when practiced indirectly versus directly. When practiced indirectly, you have the virtues that are exemplified by the Spartans. When at war, the Spartans are both moderate and just, but it is war that makes them this way (1334a26–28). The extreme circumstances make it so they cannot survive if they do not practice both of them: one does not make a free choice to be moderate or just in warfare; you simply do not have the opportunity to practice vice.

Aside from the moderation and justice required indirectly for leisure—that is, the moderation and justice required for war—there is a form of these virtues that is required directly. It is the direct forms of moderation and justice that the Spartans do not have (1334a40–b5). These direct forms are what keep leisured cities from overextending themselves. Without them, Spartans become "arrogant" (1334a28). They enjoy the success they earn in warfare and begin to treat that success and its resulting spoils as the true end of warfare. The moderation and justice practiced in peace is therefore the more difficult form to cultivate (1334a27–34). Success has a way of tempting cities into a lack of moderation, and, in turn, the lack of moderation begets injustice. If a city uses its wealth immoderately, it will need to obtain more. The tried and true way of obtaining more is through the imperial rule over others.

For these reasons, Aristotle nearly goes so far as to suggest that the moderation and justice exercised in warfare are not, in fact, true examples of those virtues: "War compels them to be just and behave with moderation, while the enjoyment of good fortune and being at leisure in peacetime tend to make them arrogant" (1334a26–28). And later: "It is disgraceful not to be capable of using good things, it is still more so to be incapable of using them in leisure, but to be seen to be good men while occupied and at war but servile when remaining at peace and being at leisure" (1334a36–40). In a sense, it is *more* vicious to be the Spartans, who only practice the virtues of moderation and justice when at war, than residents of a city that never practices those virtues at all. The true test of these virtues is whether and to what extent they are practiced when in peace—when one is not compelled to practice them, but when one has a choice to practice them and practice them for the right reasons. This matches up with one of Aristotle's definitions of virtue in the *Nicomachean Ethics*: "With the things that come about as a result of the virtues, just because they themselves are a certain way it is not the case that one does them justly or temperately, but only if the one doing them also does them being a certain way: if one does them first of all knowingly, and next, having chosen them and chosen for their own sake, and third, being in a stable condition and not able to be moved all the way out of it" (*Nicomachean Ethics* 1105a29–35).[13] The Spartan forms of

20 | Leisure

moderation and justice fail at least two components of the rubric: having chosen them and having chosen them for their own sake. The Spartans, Aristotle notes, only practiced the "virtues" under compulsion and did not choose them. And to the extent that they did choose them, they did not choose them for their own sake. Had they done so, they would have been able to continue practicing them in peace and leisure. Therefore, not only do some of the virtues take on a different flavor when practiced in war and occupation versus peace and leisure, it is peace and leisure that provides the true test of those virtues.

What the Spartans seem to miss most of all is the crowning virtue of philosophy, which is the primary virtue that is directly required for leisure without also being required for war and occupation (*Politics* 1334a23–25). The lack of other, moral, virtues is in large part a lack of understanding. The Spartans come to understand the goods they gain from warfare to be greater than both attaining the virtues and being leisured (1334b1–5). In order to be truly leisured, we therefore require this virtue of philosophy. Notice that we do not need philosophy because it is the proper activity of leisure. That is not Aristotle's claim here. Instead, it seems we need philosophy to come to the intellectual recognition that the purpose of war and occupation is peace and leisure. On this, I largely agree with Solmsen and Lord that Aristotle likely intends "philosophy" here in a broad sense.[14] Given the later treatment of music as, in some forms at least, proper to the life of leisure (1339b11–20), Aristotle cannot mean only the philosopher is capable of leisure, especially since the discussion is of virtues held at the city level, not just those of some of its inhabitants. However, I will not broaden it as widely as Lord, who argues for it in the sense of "culture."[15] This is because it remains a virtue in this context, and this suggests more than a collective interest in the fine arts, but also an intellectual *aptitude*. Perhaps Aristotle does not require theoretical virtue to the level of Socrates, but, as suggested earlier, it at least implies the ability to recognize that war is for the sake of peace, and occupation is for the sake of leisure.[16] Regardless of the precise level of specificity that Aristotle intends by using philosophy as a virtue in this context, the larger point remains: leisure itself requires virtues, both of the moral and intellectual variety.

Where does this discussion of virtues required for leisure get us in terms of the final thesis of leisure as a way of being? Quite far, I think. It shows that leisure is far more substantial than the mere absence of work. It is difficult to achieve and it is the proper end of the aforementioned virtues, whether directly or indirectly. It is not whenever I *happen* to be free from occupation but something I *cultivate*. If leisure were merely free time, or even also including the material equipment necessary for leisure, the Spartans would be leisured or capable of leisure. And yet, Aristotle argues that they are not. They lack the ability because they lack the true forms of moderation and justice, and, especially, the virtue of philosophy that is required in order to recognize peace and leisure as the proper end of all of their war and occupation.

Aristotle's discussion of the virtues required for leisure also supports the interpretation of leisure as a "way of being" because it shows it to be separate from other ways of being. As we saw, there is not a perfect overlap in the virtues required for leisure and those for occupation. Leisure has additional requirements, most notably the virtue of philosophy, but even the virtues that do happen to overlap are not quite the same for the warlike and the peaceful. Aristotle shows that the moderation practiced in war can be radically different from the moderation practiced and required for peace and leisure. It may be objected that Aristotle's inclusion of additional virtues in the life of leisure, as well as it being the ground of a higher expression of overlapping virtues such as moderation, does not suggest different ways of being so much as a more excellent expression of the human being. These are not exclusive explanations. The life of war and the life of leisure can be different ways of being in addition to their being in an hierarchical relationship. Both lives require excellences, and to some extent they are competing. They are different ways of being, and the way of leisure is concluded to be superior.

Leisure as an End

One of the conclusions that follows from the preceding discussion is that leisure has a complex relationship with the virtues. Leisure, in the sense most commentators refer to, is required to develop the virtues. But, as we saw, the virtues are themselves required in order to achieve leisure in the highest sense. Making matters more complicated is that leisure requires particular virtues over others. What explains this difference, I believe, is that the life of leisure and the life of politics and moral virtue are, to a significant degree, different lives. In fact, this misunderstanding regarding the fundamental tension between the political and the theoretical life seems to be why some commentators only see half of what Aristotle means by

22 | Leisure

leisure. For instance, Owens portrays the moral life and the theoretical life as one and the same, because they both partake in the virtues, which coincides with treating leisure as largely a precondition to theoretical wisdom.[17] Taking into consideration Aristotle's critique of political virtue, though, makes us better able to see this concept in its fullest expression.[18]

The way Aristotle relates leisure and politics is seemingly contradictory. In some places, Aristotle clearly states that leisure is required, as a means, for the political life (1331b40–32a2). However, in other places, especially in the *Nicomachean Ethics*, Aristotle suggests that the political life is unleisured (1177b5–20).[19] One simple way to explain this seeming contradiction is that leisure is required to attain the virtues necessary to succeed in politics, but the political life is itself busy and lacks leisure. While this is true in a sense, it does not fully capture Aristotle's nuanced use of leisure. This is because the political life does not lack leisure simply because it takes a lot of time; it is unleisurely because it is not a final end. There are certainly more and less noble ways of living the political life. The rule over slaves is far less noble than the skillful rule over the free and virtuous, for instance (*Politics* 1333b26–28). But even political rule over the free and virtuous is not a final end. It is still *for* something else; that something else being leisure.

The preceding suggests a particular interpretation of the fact that rule in Aristotle's ideal regime is by rotation (1329a15–16).[20] Because Greek political life demanded so much time and resources from its citizens,[21] rotation allowed citizens to have stints of leisure that could be uncorrupted by participation in politics. This is opposed, or is at least a supplement, to other reasons why rule might be by rotation: because of an equality among the class of those that are citizens, or because justice demands that citizens each have an opportunity to enjoy and display political virtue. Recognizing leisure as an end suggests that rotation is instituted so that citizens can enjoy and cultivate a life outside and above politics.

According to the current interpretation, then, the political life takes a back seat to the life of leisure. But this raises a further, obvious, question: Why should citizens be involved in politics at all? If leisure is the proper end of the good life, why should citizens be bothered by politics? Why not relegate the tasks of governing to others in the same way labor is relegated to noncitizens? Further evidence of Aristotle's "realism,"[22] even when discussing his ideal regime, is his awareness that wisdom in politics is required in order to secure and sustain a city devoted to ends beyond politics.[23] A fully leisured city may be ideal, but, in the same way that a life completely composed of contemplation is not practicable for the human being (*Nicomachean Ethics* 1177b16–78a2), a fully leisured city, without any concern for politics, cannot exist. Political participation is still required of leisured citizens because they alone are capable of seeing the true end of politics in a way those devoted to politics and ruling over others, such as the Spartans, are incapable of. Aristotle does not, primarily, place the responsibility of knowing the true ends of human life on the shoulders of individuals. Instead, the responsibility is placed on the shoulders of political leaders (1333a37–40).[24] As we saw earlier, citizens need to be directed toward the appropriate activities of noble leisure. This education is not a private one, and this way of life needs to be cultivated by the regime. Participation by rotation, therefore, is an attempt to solve the following problem: only those that are leisured are capable of the highest forms of political rule, but political rule is itself not leisured. Rotation attempts to solve this by allowing citizens freedom from politics, while also taking advantage of the unique virtues only the leisured possess.

The following question remains: Will not the enlightened citizens of this ideal regime eschew politics because of its lower status? Or, in the very least, will they refuse to take the activity seriously? Though Aristotle does not, on my account, view the political life as the highest expression of human excellence, it nevertheless enjoys a relatively high status. As Yack artfully puts it, the political life is qualified by Aristotle but not rejected.[25] Political activity is in no danger of sinking, in Aristotle's ranking, to the level of, say, artisanship. And again, political rule in the ideal regime is rule over other free citizens, which is inherently nobler than other forms of rule. Finally, the political life also shares in theoretical wisdom, at least in its highest expressions.[26] It requires debates and ruminations over questions of justice and the best life. Politicians need to be aware of the true end of politics and human life in order to lead adequately. Otherwise, the means can all too easily be mistaken for the end. Thus, though the political life is not the highest expression of human excellence, it is close; and good, thoughtful, politicians are necessary to secure the highest lives for the citizens of their city.[27]

Leisure as an end is further elaborated in in book 8 of the *Politics*, where the subject of education returns to the forefront. There we receive a direct questioning of the true and ideal activity to be practiced in leisure. One possible activity, play, is the first to be dismissed (1337b32–36). Play is for the sake of rest and is merely a remedy for the tension to be found in occupation. Consider how, when we take time away from work, we use

24 | Leisure

the phrase "recharge our batteries." What is implied by that statement is that rest and play restore us for something else, and that something else is most likely work. Play is therefore not the *end* of occupation but in fact *serves* occupation. Meanwhile, leisure is "held itself to involve pleasure, happiness, and living blessedly" (1338a1–3). Play and leisure seem to share pleasure, but play does not share, at least as completely, in happiness and "living blessedly." On the relationship between work, play, and leisure, Solmsen provides a helpful and precise characterization. Instead of treating work and play as opposites, Aristotle sees them as two sides of the same coin. Play serves work, while leisure does not and is an end in itself. Thus, instead of depicting the two as different categories, with leisure associated with play, Aristotle lumps work and play together, with leisure as a separate category.[28] Aristotelian leisure therefore transcends this dichotomy between work and play.

The next hint given by Aristotle is that leisure is "not available to those who are occupied" (1338a3–7). Though Aristotle may initially seem to be relying upon the dichotomy of work and leisure, the very one just dismissed, a careful reading of the passage suggests otherwise. Notice that the lack of occupation is not equated with leisure. Instead, the lack of occupation is a mere precondition to leisure. This freedom is necessary to leisure, but the freedom from labor does not completely compose it. Furthermore, the way in which the freedom from occupation is connected to leisure is quite different from our own understanding. The reason why freedom from occupation is required for leisure is that those who are occupied are "occupied for the sake of some end that is assumed not to be present" (1338a4–5). Recalling the connection made between leisure and *energeia*, it is in leisure that the end is present. Leisured activity can involve motion, but it is a motion that is always achieving its end. Still further, occupation is accompanied by pain, while leisure is pleasurable. However, though pleasurable, leisure requires a lot of us. It requires particular virtues, such as courage and endurance (indirectly) and moderation and justice (directly). Leisure also requires a substantial amount of time; more than the time available to those who work. It is therefore a serious endeavor that requires dedication. The farmer cannot engage in leisured activity, nor can he "be at leisure," despite Aristotle's recognition that farmers have free time after the harvest (*Nicomachean Ethics* 1160a26–30). It is a way of life that is only available to those that are fortunate enough to have the necessary equipment and are virtuous enough to engage in the activities proper to it.

Though Pieper incorporates some of these elements of leisure, especially the transcendence from the dichotomy of work and play,[29] his account remains focused on festivity.[30] To the extent that this festivity transcends its use for recovering one from labor, Pieper's account of leisure may approach leisure as a way of being, especially with its connection to the creation of culture,[31] but it remains distinct from Aristotle's understanding. Though Aristotelian leisure is pleasurable, it, on the whole, remains serious rather than playful. Virtue and an education are directed toward it, and, furthermore, it is understood as an end. Pieper gets closest when calling leisure a "condition of the soul."[32] This condition of the soul goes beyond "vacation" and "time off,"[33] but its break with the dichotomy of work and play is not as stark as it is in Aristotle. As a condition, rather than a way of being, the same people who live in the realm of work and play remain capable of leisure. Aristotle's conception is more radical, as suggested in the discussion of both the exclusion of the farmer from citizenship in the ideal regime and also of the limits of the political life. Pieper's account of leisure, though interesting on its own, does not capture or recover this spirit.

Leisure and Music

Thus far, we have yet to address the possible activities that are worthy of Aristotelian leisure. To some extent, this is the wrong question to ask. Leisure is not a particular set of activities so much as an orientation that we bring to those activities. Nevertheless, it is true that some activities are more proper and fitting than others. In the very least, we would expect the leisured to engage in activities in a different way than others without their advantages. This is why, when it comes to the particular activities proper to leisure, Aristotle does not give a direct answer. Instead, he writes: "This pleasure, however, is not regarded as the same by all, but by each individual in accordance with themselves and their own disposition; but the best sort regards it as the best pleasure and that deriving from the noblest things" (1338a6–9). This does not mean, of course, that the scope of appropriate activity is infinitely wide, in the way we would account for leisure today as "free time." Though there is some variation, the pleasure that is derived is from the "noblest things." As the highest activity, and the one that expresses the highest virtue, contemplation is an obvious contender for being worthy of leisure—of being something

26 | Leisure

that is done for its own sake and is also worthy of that devotion. But is that it? Is contemplation the sole activity that can properly be said to be undergone in leisure? If this is true, then leisure would be more or less a proxy for contemplation. Its character of being a way of being would remain, but it would be closer to a singular state or condition marked by intellectual virtue rather than a way of being. The question then becomes: What other activities are worthy of leisure, and what do those activities tell us about leisure? For this, I will turn to Aristotle's discussion of music in book 8 of the *Politics*.

The primary question concerning music is whether it is "education, play, or pastime" (1339b10–14). In different ways, music is each of those things.[34] There are then three purposes of music education, with the purposes ascending in importance and value. The first purpose, associated with play, is amusement. Amusement is pleasurable, but it is *merely* pleasurable. It is a form of rest that serves to recuperate one for later occupation. This is perhaps the most common use of music. The second purpose, associated with education, is moral virtue. In short, music affects us. It captures our emotions and is capable of pointing our emotions in different directions. The particular directions music can point us are important, as music can make us "feel affection" for either proper or improper things (1340a22–23).

The final and most important purpose, associated with pastime, is leisure. Though many commentators, such as Lord, focus on the role of music in moral education, even going so far as to lump completely the "pastime" element of music into the educative element,[35] there is an element of music appreciation that goes beyond both pleasure and moral education.[36] Leisure is the most essential and valuable purpose because it is an end in itself. Experiencing and recognizing the enjoyment of music as an end is difficult, in part because it looks much like, and is often confused for, the enjoyment of music as play. The outward presentation of both may be exactly the same. In the same way that the virtuous man is difficult to recognize because beauty of the soul is not as easily recognized as beauty of the body (1254b27–55a3), it is difficult to recognize and differentiate between someone at play and someone at leisure. Both play and leisure are pleasurable. What separates the two is whether that pleasure is animated by rest, which is merely a means to some other end, or whether the pleasure is animated by leisure, which is an end in itself. The fullest enjoyment of music, then, is that which notices and appreciates the music's beauty simply for the sake of the beautiful. Aristotle says as much when prescribing the proper mode of teaching drawing to children: "They should be educated in drawing not so that they may not make errors in their private purchases and avoid being deceived in the buying and selling of wares, but rather because it makes them expert at studying the beauty connected with bodies. To seek everywhere the element of utility is least of all fitting for those who are magnanimous and free" (1338b1–4). There is no end beyond recognizing and appreciating beauty. We may enjoy beauty as a rest from the toil of work and as instructive for later acts of virtue, but these are lower activities for the very reason that they serve some other purpose. The study of beauty itself, meanwhile, is not "for" anything. There are ends below it, but not above or beyond it.

The obvious contender for an appropriate activity of leisure is the highest activity—contemplation. However, Aristotle's curious section on education and music suggests that contemplation is not alone. Music, because its value goes beyond its role in the development of moral virtue, and into the appreciation of beauty, is also a contender. Aristotle does not provide an exhaustive list of appropriate activities of leisure, which is exactly consistent with the understanding of leisure developed here, but he gives us a rubric instead: they need to be capable of being undergone for their own sake, rather than as a means to some other end. It is therefore less an engagement in a particular activity and more the purpose underlying the completion of that activity and the various excellences employed along the way. This accounts for Aristotle's "failure" to enumerate directly and exhaustively the proper activities of leisure. It is, in this way, the wrong question to ask. Again, this is not to say all activities are equal. Aristotle certainly seems to preclude all that involve toil, for example. Still, there appear to be multiple acceptable manifestations of being at leisure. Philosophy and what we would now call the fine arts are clear candidates. Also, leisure seems to presuppose philosophy in that it involves the recognition of the forms—whether of beauty or truth or goodness.[37] Though other activities may suffice, studying the higher arts may be the clearest and most direct route to recognizing beauty. The same is true of philosophy for truth. This partially explains why Aristotle emphasizes the proper appreciation of music rather than skillfully playing an instrument. The playing of music is only valuable in the instrumental sense: it helps us better appreciate harmonies and melodies. Aristotelian leisure cannot therefore be reduced to an aristocratic "deeply seated prejudice,"[38] where playing for others is simply undignified. Continuing the play of music after such an ability is gained is to, once again, mistake the means for the end.

28 | Leisure

Conclusion

Inquiring into the concept of leisure forces us to address some of the most primordial and important questions: How should I spend my time, and where should I devote my energies? On my account, Aristotle conceives of leisure first as a way of being rather than a specific set of activities or as a mere precondition to those activities. Looking to the discussion of music in book 8 of the *Politics*, we see that the mere listening to music is not enough to categorize the activity as leisured. What is important is not *that* you listen to music but your specific *comportment* to the music and your *ability* to recognize and appreciate the forms of beauty in that activity. Leisure requires much. It requires time, energy, and skill. It requires skill and virtue to not only push away the use*ful* but also the ability and intellect to appreciate the use*less*. As the example of music shows, if leisure is an "activity," it is so in the sense of an *energeia*. Using music in the development of moral virtue is insufficient because it is on the way to something else. Only the leisured appreciation of beauty is a complete end. We do not, of course, have to go so far as to suggest that only the life perfectly removed from all utility is in fact leisured. As we saw, it is also improper to say that the leisured citizen is or should be perfectly uninterested in politics. However, the life of leisure understands itself as fundamentally devoted to those things that are worthy for their own sake. Political activity may be undergone, but it is now understood as valuable as a means, noble as it may be, rather than valuable as a final end.

Now that we have seen Aristotelian leisure in its fullest expression, as a way of being, we begin to accurately recognize the nature of leisure's challenge to liberal values. Because leisure is not merely the absence of occupation, or a precondition to the virtues, or even a "condition of the soul," but is instead a way of being that contradicts other ways of life, its challenge to liberalism, with liberalism's emphasis on work and commerce,[39] is different and more extreme than is implied by other common definitions of leisure. Up until this point, we have played fast and loose with this term, "liberalism." I have associated it with the general tendency of valuing work. If classical leisure challenges liberal values, our next task must be to better understand those liberal values that are supposedly being contradicted. Once we have done so, we will be in a better position to understand the shape any potential future leisure may take.

Chapter 2

Locke on the Necessity of
Labor for Happiness

Introduction

In telling the story of leisure, we must account for its downfall. Leisure may have been valued by the Greek philosophers and later European aristocrats, but somewhere along the way, minds were changed. This chapter is an account of one particularly forceful, and influential, rejection of leisure in favor of work. It is not the only rejection, but given John Locke's central place in the liberal tradition that continues to influence us today, he is representative of the liberal response to the Aristotelian tradition of leisure. Because of its influence, it is the liberal tradition that must be encountered, and itself either rejected or adapted, if leisure is to regain a significant stature.

If leisure is to be valued, it is primarily because of its supposed relationship with human fulfillment. Meanwhile, our arguments in favor of work and labor are typically incommensurable with this line of thinking. Arguments in favor of work and labor tend to focus on issues of equality or freedom. When we tell the story of labor in liberalism, we are apt to say that labor should be privileged because of fairness, or because of its relationship to natural rights. We can still make leisure and labor face one another, but the debate will not be commensurable; it will instead be the weighing of different principles. There is value in this, but it would be better, or at least more complete, if we could make leisure and labor use the same language and answer the same questions.

30 | Leisure

It is not just that we often *ignore* the pieces of liberal thought that deal with questions of fulfillment, happiness, and virtue, but there is also a tendency to *deny* that they were ever there. There is a lively debate about the extent to which liberalism is or should be neutral when it comes to notions of the good life.[1] However, in this debate over *whether* notions of the good exist or belong in the liberal tradition, the *content* of the liberal good is rarely systematically treated. And insofar as the content of it is treated, which is typically done within the context of liberal virtues,[2] those accounts focus on the importance of certain virtues for the vitality of liberal government and ignore the role those virtues play in individual human happiness.[3] For instance, we might say that tolerance is a virtue of a liberal citizen, but primarily because that person helps make for a society more consistent with liberal political goals. But that does not answer whether such a virtue, or any others, make the individual happy. As Tomasi puts it, most accounts of liberal virtue see virtue as "derivative" of the public good.[4] This chapter follows the lead of those like Tomasi that see liberalism providing a fuller "ethical background culture."[5] I seek to highlight the conception of the good life found in the writing of Locke. Instead of stopping at what Locke thinks creates *public* happiness, I address how liberal virtues make claims to creating *private* felicity.

While I will discuss Locke's account of happiness generally, I will, for obvious reasons, emphasize the role of labor. Locke enlarges and elevates the role of labor, and he provides one of the most forceful and impactful accounts of its role in human life.[6] However, even if we accept labor as the legitimate basis of property, it can still be the case that labor is fundamentally a painful and unsatisfying aspect of our condition. On this account, labor is useful, but it is an unavoidable evil. And this is how many, such as Alan Ryan and Jeremy Waldron, interpret Locke.[7] So the story goes, labor is painful, but it creates value, which makes for safer and freer political communities. Again, the focus is on political goods. Contra this interpretive tradition, I defend an interpretation of Locke that sees labor as not simply a curse but also a source of fulfillment. Though labor as a source of fulfillment is typically associated with later Hegelian and Marxist traditions, I suggest that early liberalism can account for labor as more than the painful source of property. Indeed, if such an account of labor were missing from Lockean liberalism, this would be a strike against it. If we understand property as Locke does, as a necessary component of preservation,[8] and if labor, as opposed to inheritance or charity, is the primary legitimate foundation of property, it would be problematic if labor were simply or even largely painful or corrupting. But if Locke can account for this other side of the question of labor, Lockean liberalism becomes more defensible. In the very least, such an account provides a more complete retelling of the liberal tradition with which leisure needs to contend.

The movement of the following is a narrowing down. To link labor with happiness, I begin with aligning Lockean happiness with self-authorship. Self-authorship, we find, requires labor. This labor comes in at least three forms: physical, cognitive, and occupational. Physical labor, for Locke, is more than an analogy for the other types. As others have noticed, Locke uses the metaphors of business and industry rather gratuitously.[9] However, the following argues that the significance of this language goes beyond metaphor. In a way that radically separates him from previous thinkers, Locke finds even intellectual activity, and the pleasure that is associated with it, to be marked by labor and industry. Even further, occupational and physical labor is a source of pleasure and is *required* for happiness as Locke understands it. Though I cite widely from Locke's corpus, the following is largely a study of the *Essay Concerning Human Understanding*[10] and *Some Thoughts Concerning Education*,[11] two works of Locke's that, despite some growing interest over the last few decades, remain largely ignored by political theorists.[12]

In focusing on the argument for labor from the standpoint of happiness, I am not suggesting that Locke is somehow unconcerned with equality and freedom. Instead, I am arguing that the relationship between labor and happiness must be remembered to tell the full story of liberalism, especially in its rejection of leisure. Even further, Locke's account of happiness is consistent with, and even underlies, his concern for equality and freedom. To bring this out, I end the chapter with a discussion of Frederick Douglass, whose account of the evils of slavery is consistent with a liberal notion of the good life.

Labor as a Curse

There is some good reason to believe that Locke would hold labor to be a painful curse, despite its role as the legitimate origin of property. First, the position makes intuitive sense and corresponds to much everyday

32 | Leisure

experience. Much of our labor is done, not because it is a source of joy or fulfillment to us, but because it is instrumentally valuable. Whether it be pay or something else, many of us only engage in work and labor because of some other desired result. Even if we agree with Locke that work, rather than inheritance or charity, is the legitimate origin of property, we also recognize this potentially negative characteristic of labor—its instrumental quality. Without a promise of some beneficial conclusion to labor, we would not do it. This orientation to labor assumes that labor is necessarily painful, or is at least the source of unease.

Because some of Locke's treatment of labor corresponds with this orientation—indeed, much of our orientation, especially labor as the origin of property, is *due* to Locke—it would be reasonable for Locke to also view labor as a kind of curse. However, this interpretive view is largely an assumption that is indulged in rather than a conclusion that is demonstrated. For instance, both Ryan and Waldron make the claim in passing as if it did not require a defense.[13] According to Ryan, the view that work is fulfilling comes after Locke, finding form in Hegel and early Marx. Hegel saw the work as a form of self-expression and as the primary way of humanizing and even creating the world.[14] Though Ryan does not give a full account of the relative misery or joy found in Lockean labor, it is assumed that it is not present. It is a later development to be found in the "Romantic" theory of ownership, not in liberalism's early founders such as Locke. Only later do we see such a "bond" between people and their property.[15] Doing better, Strauss cites a few paragraphs in the *Second Treatise* as evidence for such a view. In his provocative conclusion that Lockean happiness is a "joyless quest for joy," Strauss claims that the means of assuaging pain, which is labor, is also a pain.[16] As evidence, he cites sections of the *Second Treatise*, where, as a placeholder for labor, Locke uses the idiom "taking pains." For instance, Locke writes:

> Amongst those who are counted the civilized part of mankind, who have made and multiplied positive laws to determine property, this original law of nature, for the beginning of property, in what was before common, still takes place; and by virtue thereof, what fish any one catches in the ocean, that great and still remaining common of mankind; or what ambergrise any one takes up here, is by the labour that removes it out of that common state nature left it in, made his property, who takes that pains about it.[17]

The best evidence given for labor being the necessarily painful origin of both property and happiness is the literal reading of an idiom. The task of the following is to address this claim, and to show that it is wanting. Locke does not require all labor to be pleasurable—such a position would be absurd—but Locke's account of labor is more complicated than simply being the painful origin to property. Not only does labor form the basis of the legitimate right to property, but Locke also accounts for labor being an important and necessary component of rational self-authorship, which is itself a necessary component of happiness.

Self-Authorship and Happiness

The first step in defending labor as a necessary condition for happiness is laying bare the connection between happiness and self-authorship. Locke is a hedonist, even if of a complicated sort.[18] Roughly, he believes a happy life is one with little unease and greater amounts of pleasure. Locke's hedonism is present in both his account of happiness as well as his account of morality. While it is true that Locke differentiates between proper and improper pleasures,[19] even moral good and evil centers around pleasure and pain. The primary difference is that moral law involves rewards and punishments, and thereby pleasures and pains, resulting from obeying or disobeying moral law. Moral law therefore adds another step to the calculus but does not change its ultimate and driving principle.[20] Moral laws and virtues, then, are useful tools for attaining happiness.

What we need to answer, then, is how we achieve more pleasure than pain. Locke's answer is that we need to be "rational," which means not only choosing correctly what causes pleasure and pain but also shaping our lives so that we are *directed* by reason and its dictates, rather than irrational desires. In becoming more rational, we become self-authors rather than unfree slaves to our desires. The happiest persons, then, are those that actively shape their own lives to the greatest extent. Happiness is found in taking extreme responsibility for ourselves, not just in controlling our irrational urges but even further in *creating* ourselves. As we will see, self-authorship is not limited to the shaping of our moral lives but also our intellectual lives. In the following, the use of "self-authorship" is constituted by two parts: self-control and self-creation.

Self-control is best seen in Locke's account of the suspension of desire. True happiness is often hidden and obstructed by immediate desire,

34 | Leisure

and rationality and self-authorship is what is activated in the suspension of that desire.[21] Locke, of course, is not unique in requiring self-control in the pursuit of happiness. However, Locke does not stop at self-control but also prescribes self-creation. This is where his position is much more novel. We will later connect it to occupational forms of labor, but Locke's prescription for self-creation is seen most clearly in his epistemology, both in his rejection of innate ideas and in his account of disengagement. First, on the rejection of innate ideas, Locke's position is found in the answer to the following question: How do I come to know the sources of good and evil understood as pleasure and pain? Locke answers emphatically that reason, as opposed to innate ideas, are our source of knowledge. This is true not only of knowledge generally but also of moral knowledge.[22] Nature furnishes us with an inclination for happiness and an aversion to misery, but it does not furnish us with ideas about how to achieve it. Nature gives us the goal, as well as some faculties and tendencies that help direct us, but nature does not provide the means. Because of this lack of instinct, we are capable of a wide variety of thoughts and desires. The problem is that not all ideas and desires lead us well. Our thoughts are "more than the sands, and wider than the ocean where fancy and passion must needs run him into strange courses," and our imagination is "always restless, and suggests variety of thoughts, and the will, reason being laid afield, is ready for every extravagant project."[23] Our various thoughts, imaginations, and desires can lead us into a wide array of activity, experience, and understandings of the good. In other words, we can become quite strange and miserable creatures if left to our own devices. The natural perfect freedom we find in the state of nature finds a corollary in the untrained mind. Luckily, we have another faculty that, though not as powerful as instinct, is our means of giving direction to the seemingly infinite diversity of ideas, imaginations, and desires. This faculty, of course, is reason, which is our "only star and compass."[24] Reason is able to put together, compare, sort out, and order the ideas that are otherwise without order. We may not be able to stop the constant motion of ideas and sensations, but we are able to give them a pattern and accept or reject those that are respectively coherent or incoherent. In this way, our lack of instinct is a kind of blessing but also operates as a potential source of corruption and gives human beings an increased responsibility.[25] As is shown in *Some Thoughts Concerning Education*, there is a place for authority in setting up the right habits and virtues,[26] but ultimately it is individual reason that must guide us. Many of those habits created through the authority of parents, for instance, are in the service of developing reason in the pupil. Even more importantly, rationality is best understood here as a form of self-creation. As rational corporeal creatures, we are ultimately responsible for our own selves.[27] Part of this responsibility is sorting out what makes us happy.

It is not just the lack of innate ideas that points toward self-creation but also Locke's radical espousal of disengagement. In the modern era, as Taylor points out, it is not until Locke that the ideas of disengagement and rational control reach their full expression.[28] Taylor goes so far as to say that Locke's view of knowledge as sense experience, in opposition to innate ideas and various forms of rationalism, was not as radical as was his view of disengagement.[29] Other traditions, including the Thomistic, also give weight to sense experience over innate ideas. What is far more unique, then, is the extent to which Locke thinks we can "disengage" from nearly all of our mental activity. We begin from the one mental component that is largely *not* in our control: simple ideas. Though we have some impact over simple ideas, the understanding is largely passive in this regard.[30] We simply take in, through sense experience, these simple ideas. While we do not have a large hand in these basic building blocks, we can construct them in a variety of ways. This is because simple ideas cannot do much on their own. We need to create complex ideas, which, unlike their simple counterparts, are not passively entered into our minds. These complex ideas are *created* through the combination and organization of simple ideas. In other words, we have to construct a world ourselves, using these building blocks.[31] There is, then, another corollary between the operations of our mind and the creation of property. The mind, much like land in the state of nature, is not of much use to us on its own. Land requires cultivation in order to be productive. It is not what is given to us, the commons, that is valuable, it is what our labor introduces to the land that makes it valuable. Labor, as opposed to nature, is responsible for at least 99 percent of all value.[32] The same is true of our minds. That which is given to us, simple ideas, is not of much use. We have work to do. This work, which Taylor calls the reification of the mind,[33] is the uniting and separating of simple ideas.

We become responsible, then, not only for our own material well-being but also our happiness and the relative accuracy of our view of the external world.[34] Galston, following Rogers Smith, calls Lockean responsibility "rational self-direction."[35] But even this is not enough. Rational self-direction would be fitting if Locke were only interested in the direction we give ourselves in terms of the establishment of values

36 | Leisure

and the development of the various virtues that help us achieve the kind of life we choose. Locke certainly attributes such responsibility to us. But, considering the aforementioned, we are required to have control over more than our desires. We are also in charge of the shape of our minds. It is complex ideas that are important, and how we put together these simple ideas is under our control. This is why I find "rational self-direction" to not go far enough and find rational self-*authorship* to be more fitting. It is not enough to control unruly desires, but we must also *create* ourselves. We must create our material well-being through the mixing of labor with the inadequate given of nature, and likewise we must shape our minds through the combining and ordering of the inadequate given of simple ideas.

Work and Self-Authorship

So far, we have seen that happiness requires self-authorship. Self-authorship is understood in terms of both self-control and self-creation. The next step is to look more closely at how this self-authorship is achieved. I will argue that it requires work, of its cognitive, occupational, and even physical varieties. Beginning with cognitive labor, Locke connects work and industriousness with our capacity to reason in multiple ways. First, being rational is not a form of idleness but is active and requires industry: "The wise and considerate men of the world, by a right and careful employment of their thoughts and reason, attained true notions in this, as well as other things; whilst the lazy and inconsiderate part of men, making the far greater number, took up their notions, by chance, from common tradition and vulgar conceptions without much beating their heads about them."[36] Reason requires ingenuity. Though we cannot stop ideas from moving in and out of our minds, our will can direct our minds in particular directions. The cognitive laziness described by Locke is not a lack of movement but is instead an avoidance of critical thought. Ideas are always in motion, but it is up to the relative industriousness of the individual to assess whether those ideas correspond to reality and whether they cohere or contradict other accepted ideas. The mind is always receiving sensations, but the practice of thinking is unnecessary.[37] This is partly why, in *Some Thoughts Concerning Education*, Locke describes laziness in children as a "sickness."[38] If reason is required for true and stable happiness, and if reason requires industriousness, then laziness inevitably leads to misery. Without an industriousness of the mind, the individual becomes a slave to mere immediate cures of unease and is unable to secure a more lasting and higher happiness.

Cognitive labor is not only involved in avoiding moral vice, but it is also necessary to the higher intellectual virtues. The faculty of understanding, in particular, is a source of enjoyment. In fact, it is the source of the highest and most stable pleasures: "*the* UNDERSTANDING, *who does not know, that as it is the most elevated faculty of the soul, so it is employed with a greater, and more constant delight than any of the others.*"[39] The relationship between the understanding and happiness is more direct than it is in the case of moral self-control. In the suspension of desire, reason is connected to joy in a rather remote or instrumental way. Suspension is not by necessity pleasurable on its own. In fact, it may be painful. It implies, at least temporarily, the refusal to give in to a desire, a desire that may be strongly felt. Not only is the refusal of desire uneasy, but so is the desire itself.[40] Suspension implies both the desire and its refusal, both of which are uneasy. The promise of suspension is the possibility of greater joy or lack of unease in the future, but this means its value is instrumental or at least remote from its actual practice. The pleasure of the understanding, meanwhile, is direct and can be immediate.

Importantly, it is the *working* of the faculty of the understanding that is joyful, regardless of its conclusion. We do not need to arrive at a unifying theory of the universe in order to feel such pleasure: "*Its searches after truth, are a sort of hawking and hunting, wherein the very pursuit makes a great part of the pleasure.*"[41] Though the use of the understanding implies a level of competence, the joy of its practice does not require the attainment of truth. Contra Aristotelian contemplation, where the aim is the *having* of truth, it is the *pursuit* that is enjoyable. The significance of this point is difficult to overstate. Newton is not happiest when he arrives at the conclusion of his experiment but during the experimentation. The philosopher of Plato's cave finds the purest joy in wresting herself free of her chains, not in the sunbathing at the cave's exit. And this wresting oneself free is a labor. Again, it is a cognitive labor, but it is a labor nonetheless.

Even if we accept that Locke includes activity of the mind as a form of labor, we may complain that the "labor" found in contemplation is not what we normally have in mind when thinking of work, even if we grant that Lockean contemplation is more laborious than Aristotelian contemplation. Locke, however, does not stop at the cognitive labor found in contemplation, or even in the suspension of desire, but also has in mind forms of labor that better conform with contemporary usage of "work."

38 | Leisure

It is what I will refer to as "occupational" labor. Here, we need to look more closely at *Some Thoughts Concerning Education*. The explicit purpose of Locke's prescribed education is to prepare the pupil for his calling.[42] The conceptual history of the calling is long and multifaceted, and Locke seems to incorporate disparate elements. As Dunn points out, Locke uses the term in at least two different senses: a particular calling and a general calling.[43] The general calling refers to our religious responsibilities, while the particular calling refers to our more or less secular responsibility to secure our comfortable passage through this world.[44] Though Dunn argues that Locke is a largely religious thinker, Locke's separation of the particular and general calling suggests that he is, in the very least, interested in separating the concerns of a profession from our religious duties. Furthermore, in his educational writings, most of Locke's concern resides with preparing the pupil for his particular rather than general calling. And as Marshall has shown, the notion of a calling already gained secular connotations by Locke's time.[45] Thus, the end of the pupil's education, even of an aristocrat,[46] is occupation. We need to address the significance of this and can do this by asking: What is the other option? What is Locke rejecting in educating the pupil for a calling? The other primary option is preparation for leisure, and the choice between these two options is a real one. The pupil in Locke's education is a member of the gentry and, as such, has access to leisure. Locke rejects this life and does so in an extreme way. The pupil not only does not have access to leisure as an adult, but he is to learn a trade, which Locke admits is an extreme position.[47] Also, the pupil is allowed recreation, but that recreation must have some utility.[48] Even more radically, the child is made to make his own toys![49] Leisure is not, as it is in Aristotle, the end of all occupation and even the end of the ideal regime (*Politics*, 1333a11–b5), but it is instead associated with vice. Whereas Aristotle found labor to be corrupting, Locke flips this on its head: labor makes us happy and leisure is the corrupting influence.

The most important critique of the leisured, then, is not their moral vacuity but is instead that the leisured are unhappy in comparison to those that work. Locke's rejection of leisure in favor of labor, then, is not simply the dour finger-wagging preacher's admonition that "idle hands are the devil's workshop." Locke understands happiness as pleasure, and if he is to advocate work over leisure, he needs to demonstrate that work is a greater source of pleasure than leisure. We can debate the extent to which his arguments are sound, but we must first recognize that they exist. First, Locke points to the anxiety of leisure.[50] A lack of activity is not pleasurable. Children prefer activity,[51] and this Locke takes to be evidence of a natural inclination of our species to prefer activity over inactivity. Idle hands, therefore, are anxious hands. They prefer to be put to use. Second, Locke argues that leisure is an idleness associated with "dice and drink." If we do not have recourse to a useful activity, we are more likely to turn to base habits. This operates as a kind of rejection of the Aristotelian premise that, given the opportunity and right education, people will generally turn to impressive activity, whether it be music or philosophy, in their free time.[52] Locke rejects this. And remember, Locke only has the English gentry in mind here, so Locke's assumption is that even those with the opportunity to remain removed from labor and receive a thorough and demanding education will turn to lower pleasures if given the opportunity. Locke, then, is in some agreement with those who say idle hands are the devil's workshop, but for Locke, the devil is simply your own future unease.

Happiness is found in and is the result of activity, but of what kind? Consistent with the pleasure found in the hawking and hunting of the intellect, Locke also finds there to be pleasure in occupation. Here is where the "labor as a curse" position must be rejected. It is not just the result of that occupation, whether it be property or something else, that gives us pleasure, but the work itself. We see this in Locke's argument that even physical labor has the capacity for pleasure. Physical labor, for the member of the gentry, forms his recreation. Recreation is "not being idle (as everyone may observe) but easing the wearied part by change of business."[53] Recreation is not complete relaxation but the relaxation of one part while exercising another. Further, the exercising of another part is not to be useless, in either the high or low sense of the word, but is to be useful. Engaging in useless activity, such as "idle sports in fashion," is not for the "rational man." Seeing oneself above useful activity is mere "vanity and pride of greatness."[54] Lockean recreation is also useful in this abstract way, but it is also intended to be directly useful. One reason to learn gardening, for instance, is so that the gentleman will be better able to direct his gardeners. Likewise, learning carpentry has the benefit of creating useful and beautiful things.[55]

Useful recreation, unlike pure idleness, has the benefit of causing future pleasure. But, again, this does not mean that Lockean recreation must be solely interested in those *future* pleasures. There is also an *immediate* pleasure found in the labor of farming and hunting. These activities may also involve some discomfort, but Locke still assumes, and requires, that

40 | Leisure

each of these forms of recreation will be enjoyable. Perhaps our bodies become sore because of the physical activity associated with carpentry or hunting, but Locke claims that such unease is overshadowed by the activity's capacity for greater joy. We only need to look at examples of "men of the greatest condition" to see that these laborious activities are a source of "constant recreation."[56]

Utility and Self-Authorship

There is a pleasure, therefore, found in work, whether it be the work of the intellect, the work of "accounts," or the work of the hands. Further, aside from some kinds of immediate gratification, many kinds of work lead to even greater future gratification. However, this still does not fully capture the role of work and labor in Locke's account of human happiness. It is also the case that it is a necessary component of the self-authorship that was delineated in the first half of this chapter. We will examine this question in light of Locke's rejection of a certain kind of aristocracy and, more importantly, *why* Locke rejects it. The question is this: Why would it be required, in an aristocratic society, that the nobility learn to create their own means of ease and safety? It is much easier to see why this would be required in a democracy where inheritance does not create a stable class of people that are free from the work that produces the means of preservation.[57] Locke's account of labor as necessary to moral virtue and happiness could be seen as limited to more or less democratic societies. The answer to this question has already been alluded to in previous discussions, but it will be addressed more directly in what remains. It can be resolved through the examination of the more specific question of whether and why a pupil should cultivate an ability to produce the means of their own security and contentment, even if that pupil has access to those goods without working for them. The question of *whether* Locke thinks the pupil should cultivate an ability to produce their own means of security is easily, and has already been, answered. Locke's *Some Thoughts Concerning Education* is written explicitly for the English gentry, precisely the class that does not need such a skill. So, *that* Locke thinks it important to be actively involved in such concerns is easily settled. The interesting and more difficult question is *why* Locke thinks this is the case. First, as we have seen, learning a trade prepares the pupil for the later management of the estate—learning to tend a garden will help the student later manage

Locke on the Necessity of Labor for Happiness | 41

his gardeners. Still, though learning a trade may help in this way, it does not form a complete answer to the question. Surely, as Locke clearly notes, this is not intended to be the "chief end of his labor." Learning a trade is meant to be a diversion from his "more serious thoughts and employments."[58] The difference between better and worse forms of recreation is whether it is marked by rational self-authorship. Drinking and gambling are irrational forms of removing unease, whereas gardening and joinery are rational. They "ease the wearied part" by removing the pupil from his study and employ his body to a task. Each activity has a goal that is being sought, and that goal should be of some use to the pupil, argues Locke.[59] Part of what separates gardening and hunting from idle sports and gambling is that the result of the activity is something of use. However, it is not simply that it is of use, but that the pupil himself was the author of that useful result. The gardener could assuredly tend tomatoes as well or better than the young gentleman, but Locke prescribes the activity anyway. Thus, Locke wants us, paradoxically, to focus on utility, *even when it is not all that useful.*

More instructive than the example of recreation is the example of the calling. Immediately after discussing the role of the trade, Locke discusses the pupil learning accounts.[60] This skill will be of more direct use for the pupil when he comes to manage an estate. But Locke believes there to be a continuity between the kinds of work. As opposed to the view that manual labor is corrupting and fundamentally distinct from noble professions and responsibilities fitting of a gentleman, Locke places them side by side and suggests, in the very least, a family resemblance. What all of this tends to is a radical taking control of one's life, including its material needs. Though Locke suggests that labor can be alienated,[61] and the pupil's eventual calling will almost certainly not be largely composed of manual labor, the calling remains best understood as the mark and practice of rational self-responsibility, self-direction, and self-creation.

The focus on rational self-responsibility is also present in the *Second Treatise.* The work of the "wise and godlike" prince is to "secure protection and encouragement to the honest industry of Mankind."[62] Notice that the work of the wise and godlike prince is not to provide material well-being for citizens. If felicity were simply the having of material possessions that give us pleasure, this would be the goal of the wise and godlike prince. Instead, the goal is to inspire industriousness.[63] When viewed in this light, Locke's critique of aristocracy is founded not upon a concern for equality but instead a concern for supporting productive industry in opposition

42 | Leisure

to aristocratic idleness.[64] It is not abundance simply that makes such an arrangement desirable but the direct relationship between industriousness and felicity. Industriousness not only has public benefits found in national abundance, but it also has private benefits in the form of felicity.

I will respond to one more possible objection. The objection is this: if it is true that labor is pleasant and that it is required in the achievement of happiness, why is it that we often view labor as a burden? There are a few reasons. First, the pleasures of labor are typically mixed. That is, they are usually mixed with unease. Though Locke asserts that the activity of hunting is pleasurable, it still requires dealing with poor weather and early waking.[65] Second, as Locke claims, most of humanity is not inclined to industriousness, in part because of the mixed character of its pleasures.[66] There are seemingly easier ways of acquiring what we want, whether it be property or knowledge. The querulous and contentious can rely upon various kinds of theft to gain property, and the cognitively lazy can rely upon authority for knowledge.[67] We view labor as a burden for the same reasons that we view a healthy diet as a burden. But as we saw, these quick paths to pleasure are typically false paths. Work is required for legitimate property, true knowledge, and stable happiness.

Frederick Douglass and Freedom as Industry

Locke's rejection of leisure may seem far removed from concerns we might have today, such as the possible injustice of allowing some to be removed from the labor that the rest of us must do. Locke's concern with leisure seems to be motivated primarily by liberty, while ours is more concerned with equality. However, there is a relationship between those positions. We can see this more clearly when we take Locke's position out of the context of the English gentry and witness its influence on the American context, which will be described through Frederick Douglass's account of the radical evil of American slavery. As Myers persuasively argues, Douglass often uses the language of Locke.[68] The wrongness of slavery is not limited to its physical chains, according to Douglass, as it keeps its victims in perpetual childhood and bars them from achieving responsibility for their own lives. The enforced idleness of slaves during holidays, which Douglass describes in his *Narrative of the Life of Frederick Douglass*, overlaps with Locke's characterization of aristocratic leisure. Slaves are discouraged, or even barred, from accomplishing any useful tasks during this time and are encouraged, or even required, to drink excessively:

> Their object seems to be, to disgust their slaves with freedom, by plunging them into the lowest depths of dissipation. For instance, the slaveholders not only like to see the slave drink of his own accord, but will adopt various plans to make him drunk. One plan is, to make bets on their slaves, as to who can drink the most whisky without getting drunk; and in this way they succeed in getting whole multitudes to drink to excess. Thus, when the slave asks for virtuous freedom, the cunning slaveholder, knowing his ignorance, cheats him with a dose of vicious dissipation, artfully labelled with the name of liberty.[69]

The goal of the master is to deny and dampen any rational responsibility and, therefore, moral agency, in the slave. Enforced wanton idleness accomplishes this perpetual childhood. And it is not just wanton idleness that Douglass rejects but all lack of activity. Describing his own Sunday leisure, Douglass portrays his lack of activity as a "beast-like stupor, between sleep and wake."[70]

Like Locke, Douglass does not offer a higher form of leisure as an alternative but "useful" tasks: "The staid, sober, thinking and industrious ones of our number would employ themselves in making corn-brooms, mats, horse-collars, and baskets; and another class of us would spend the time in hunting opossums, hares, and coons."[71] Though this option was heavily discouraged by masters,[72] Douglass seems to admire those who were able to push away the opportunity for excessive idleness. And this takes us to Douglass's defense of free labor. The support for free labor can take two general forms. First, free labor can be defended as the absence of slavery. Here, it is good because it does not partake of the despotism and illegitimacy of slavery. But as we see hinted at in the depiction of enforced idleness at Christmas, Douglass also affirms a *positive* good found in free labor. It contributes to self-authorship, which is likewise both a right and a necessary component of human flourishing. After a brutal two-hour physical fight with the particularly cruel master Covey, Douglass proclaims that the fight "rekindled the few expiring embers of freedom, and revived within me a sense of my own manhood."[73] This rekindled sense of freedom and manhood is no doubt related to the hope

44 | Leisure

for eventual freedom from slavery, but it is crucial that that hope stems from the actual physical activity of Douglass's own hands.

The reclaiming of freedom and manhood through one's own hands is not limited to the achievement of freedom found in the ending of slavery, but it finds fulfillment within free labor. Even while still enslaved, Douglass tasted this freedom by being hired outside of his master's home. He was required to give part of his wages to his master, but he also paid for his own room and board and maintenance of his tools as a ship caulker: "It was a step towards freedom to be allowed to bear the responsibilities of a freeman, and I was determined to hold on upon it. I bent myself to the work of making money. I was ready to work at night as well as day, and by the most untiring perseverance and industry, I made enough to meet my expenses, and lay up a little money every week."[74] Again, it is not the absence of slavery that is the ultimate good but the freedom found in self-ownership, which includes the responsibility to take charge of our material well-being. Concerning a tendency he saw in former slaves to regard all work as a form of slavery, Douglass retorts: "You must not think that freedom means absence from work. Bear that in mind, I would impress it upon your minds, that if you would be prosperous, you must be industrious."[75] Of course, physical labor is not the only form of self-ownership, which is why Douglass also demands education: "They must continually strive to become landholders. Nor is this sufficient. They must build up schools and educate their children. Hitherto you were wont to pride yourselves on your muscle. He who could shoulder the heaviest burden was the greatest man in the neighborhood. But you need something else now. You must have mind. You must make yourselves capable of thinking as well as digging."[76]

As it was for Locke, the development of reason is a necessary, and perhaps the most important, component of self-ownership. However, responsibility for material security and comfort remains central. For this reason, Douglass, like Locke, advocated for the accumulation of property. Douglass recognized the controversy of such a prescription, but he remained more direct than Locke ever was:

> Accumulate property. This may sound to you like a new gospel. You have been accustomed to hear that money is the root of all evil; that it is hard for the rich to enter the kingdom of Heaven; that this world is of no account; that we should take no thought for tomorrow, and much more of the same sort.

Locke on the Necessity of Labor for Happiness | 45

> In answer to all which I say: that no people can ever make any social or mental improvement whose exertions are thus limited. On the other hand, property, money, if you please, will purchase for us the only condition by which any people can rise to the dignity of genuine manhood.[77]

Against the otherworldly tendency of many of those facing grave injustices, Douglass argues for a focus on this world, and not just in the direct fighting against injustices. He strongly suggests the accumulation of property, not only because greater wealth leads to greater political power and the chance to further fight unequal treatment, but also because property accumulation is both a natural right[78] and part of the "dignity of genuine manhood." If freedom is a necessary component of human flourishing, and freedom in its full flowering demands self-creation, then property accumulation is requisite of happiness. For Douglass, then, property is to be valued for both intrinsic and extrinsic reasons. It is *intrinsically* valuable because taking responsibility for our material needs and comfort is the most direct and concrete form of self-ownership. It is *extrinsically* valuable because it also supports other, perhaps higher, forms of self-ownership. Education, and the taking charge of our minds and its constituent ideas, can only take place if our material needs are satisfied. But, as it was for Locke, the intrinsic provides a limit to the extrinsic. This is to say that the extrinsic value of property accumulation can never take precedence over the intrinsic. If it were, the ultimate goal would be leisure, where we could spend more time becoming and being self-owners of our minds. This is not the goal for Douglass for much the same reason that is not for Locke. Just as Locke prescribes labor for the gentry, Douglass does not advocate leisure for its own sake, as a final end whose value supersedes all others.

Douglass does occasionally speak well of leisure, but he also suggests that "leisure" should itself be useful. We saw this in his praise of the slaves that used the holiday break to make "corn-brooms, mats, horse-collars, and baskets."[79] And in the previously quoted address in Nashville, where he directly advocates for the accumulation of property, Douglass also supports property for its role in creating leisure. But his description of that leisure is telling: "Without property, there can be no leisure. Without leisure, there can be no thought. Without thought, there can be no invention."[80] Initially, Douglass appears to support the Aristotelian position that work is for leisure. But we see that leisure itself has an end beyond it, which is thought. Aristotle may nod in some agreement, until

46 | Leisure

thought is said to be for the sake of invention. And it is here that the revolution is encapsulated. The classical ideal of leisure is inverted. Leisure remains in name, but its contents shaken out, flipped upside down, and repackaged. Leisure is no longer the end but a means—and a means to further utility. Just as leisure's meaning gets inverted, so does labor and utility. Usefulness, paradoxically, becomes the final end. This is coherent, as usefulness becomes the essence of rationality. The gentry learning a trade, that we see in Locke's education, is of dubious concrete use. But usefulness is the mark and essence of the industrious and rational, who come to inherit the Earth.[81]

Conclusion

Allowing a class of people to enjoy freedom from labor at the expense of everyone else is, to us, not only distasteful but intolerable. This is certainly part of the explanation for the downfall of leisure, but it is incomplete. There is not just an issue of justice involved in our rejection of leisure but also a theory of human happiness built into that rejection. Even further, as we see in Douglass, the rejection from a concern from justice also implies an understanding of felicity that requires work. Once we recognize the fullness of the rejection of leisure, we are in a position to better compare the claims of each, as the two ways of life are now using the same language. Any argument for leisure, such as Aristotle's, argues at the level of human fulfillment. If leisure is worth having, it is because it is a necessary component of fulfilling the best aspects of our nature. To ask whether it is fair or unfair for some to have leisure while others do not is to ask a different question, even if valuable.

For us to remember leisure, then, we must do more than achieve the necessary material means. Liberalism has created societies of great wealth. If liberalism were only concerned with matters of justice, understood as the protection of rights, we would expect leisure to thrive in a liberal society more than any other. With unprecedented resources and freedom to live as we please, you might expect many to use those resources and freedoms to leave the workplace. But, of course, the vast majority do not. What also must be overcome is the notion of human fulfillment that is strongly associated with a life of work. For Locke, it is the industrious who not only deserve material rewards but who are most capable of happiness. Leisure is not simply unjust, but it also makes for an anxious and corrupt moral life. It is lazy and refuses to engage in rational self-authorship. As Dienstag argues, "slavery is the political evil that occupies Locke the most,"[82] and there is more to slavery than the unjust violence to natural rights. Locke also uses the language of slavery to describe the personal failure to suspend desire, as well as the mental subjugation of absolute rule.[83] As with Douglass, slavery is also evil in that it keeps the subjugated in a perpetual childhood and keeps them from the human happiness found in rational self-authorship. Those that rationally self-create are simultaneously the freest and the happiest. Allowing someone to be removed from labor is unwarranted, not primarily because that would be to give that person an undue privilege, but because that person's development would be stunted. A society built on rights, likewise, is just not simply because of rights for their own sake but because such a society will potentially direct human beings toward rational self-authorship.

Locke does not offer the only account of work and labor as important to a happy life, but he is representative of the liberal tradition. Furthermore, because he is the figure most commonly associated with the concern for rights, it is useful to see that even he, of all thinkers, also provided an account of flourishing that is consistent with that concern for rights. We are not finished, however, with the story of leisure's downfall. We have taken from Locke the value of self-authorship, but we have taken it even further and made vocations the center of how we shape ourselves. It is to this radicalization of self-authorship, its relationship to our unfulfilled expectations for our careers, and what that holds for the future of leisure, that we turn to next.

Chapter 3

Vocation and the Radicalization of Labor

Introduction

Locke does the heavy lifting of inverting Aristotle's idolization of leisure in favor of work. While some find individual self-creation to be a defining feature of neoliberalism,[1] I have argued that it is present in the very origin of liberalism. Rather than being the source and ground of flourishing, leisure becomes an anxiety-filled excuse for irrational pleasure-seeking that causes more pain in the long run—and keeps us from taking charge of our lives in a rational manner. Inhabiting this position of Locke, Alain de Botton says that work focuses our anxieties on achievable goals, gives us a sense of mastery, puts food on our table, and keeps us out of trouble.[2] The conception of liberalism that I am using here, then, is not just the defense of rights but is also attached to an idea of the good life, which includes industriousness.

Despite all of Locke's heavy lifting, there is still more to our contemporary expectations of work. Locke launches much of the secular discussion of vocation, or calling, but he does not elaborate it to its fullest extent. The logic of vocation will therefore be expanded in this chapter, not simply to explain our relationship with our careers but also to ask what that means for leisure. Any "post-work" future will be the result of a reaction to our contemporary context, which is a world brimming with work. Theorizing such a future must, therefore, account for contemporary values and address which values will be conserved, which will be thrown off, and which will be revised. The goal of this chapter, then, is to do so in regard to vocation. Though I find that our attachment to vocation is

50 | Leisure

faltering, in part because vocation contains within it the seeds of its own destruction, it is also true that some of the values underlying vocation are as strong as ever. In particular, we remain strongly attached to the freedom of individuals to discover and shape themselves as they see fit, at least within the bounds of not oppressing others. The concern for autonomy and individually shaped fulfillment radicalizes Locke's account of work, in that Locke's form of freedom requires a form of rationality and obedience to law that has been shaken off. At the same time that vocation sets this as its goal, it is incapable of achieving it in most cases. The confines of a market economy—the only legitimate liberal economy—requires that most careers will not fulfill those very desires it creates.

Defining Vocation

Any serious confrontation with our values in work and vocation must address the writings of Max Weber. If we are open to leisure, it is because the rhythms of work and labor seem heartless or unfulfilling. This partly explains Weber's attempt to find the elevation of work's origin in *The Protestant Ethic and Spirit of Capitalism*. He ends his analysis by arguing that the religious foundations of such an elevation are no longer part of our psyche. Without such a foundation, we cannot expect lives devoted to a work ethic to be fulfilling. Weber suggested other foundations may have taken its place,[3] and I have attempted to lay bare one possible foundation in the ethical and epistemological thinking of Locke. For Locke, rational self-authorship is our means of becoming happy, and this is only accomplished through work.

Weber also examined the calling, or vocation, in two separate lectures: one on politics as a vocation and the other on science. In important ways, Weber is aligned with Locke, but in others, he steps beyond. He does this more fully in the vocation lectures, which is why I am turning there instead of *The Protestant Ethic and the Spirit of Capitalism*. The latter largely describes the movement and change in values that I argue finds its peak in Locke. The vocation lectures, meanwhile, go beyond the Protestant theology that Weber largely finds to be dead and attempts to describe, and also prescribe, an idea of the calling that attempts to transcend both Protestantism and capitalism. It retains and radicalizes Locke's emphasis upon self-control and self-creation, but it gives up the question of whether

Vocation and the Radicalization of Labor | 51

such a life is inherently valuable, and whether any chosen vocation can align itself with ultimate values.

Let us begin by defining terms. Though this discussion is not limited to Weber, I will rely upon Weber's simple but elegant definition of vocation. In "Politics as a Vocation," Weber finds vocation to be both a "living 'for'" and a "living 'from.'"[4] Though he initially states vocation to be *either* a living "for" or "from," Weber notes that, as a rule, it is usually both, especially in a "society based on private property."[5] As such, in the following, I will work on the assumption that vocation is both a living for and a living from.

Breaking apart this definition, the simpler component is living from. In a democratic society, all require work to support themselves materially. Tocqueville argued that this is true even of those that are wealthy.[6] Weber claims something similar: "Experience tells us that consciously or unconsciously, the concern of the well-to-do man for the economic 'security' of his own existence is a cardinal issue for the entire conduct of his life."[7] Even with significantly more security than most, the wealthy constrain their decisions with economic concerns. They may have great advantages, but they are still likely to involve themselves in activity that supports them materially. Thus, at least in democratic societies with private property, all vocations are effectively a living from.

"Living for" is the more important aspect of vocation, as it is what separates it from other experiences of work, including Aristotle's account of toil that corrupts body and soul. First, vocation requires devotion. The ultimate example of this devotion, according to Weber, is the great artist that accomplishes nothing else other than his work.[8] Though this *complete* devotion is not required, choosing the activity of one's work at the expense of other components of one's life is a necessary feature of vocation. Weber discusses this in the context of scientific vocations, but he also states this is true of other vocations such as politics.[9]

This devotion takes on a specific form—devotion to vocation as an end in itself. Consider the example of Weber's scientist.[10] The posture of the true scientist, even in light of various career frustrations and disappointments, Weber tells us, is found in the simple statement: "I live only for my 'vocation.'"[11] Though the scientist must obviously eat and have shelter, the true scientist, the one with a vocation, would pass up much better chances for material success in order to continue their work. Necessity is the true test. If you no longer required a salary from your

52 | Leisure

work, would you continue it? Only those that answer affirmatively can be said to have a vocation.

Vocation has linkages with leisure in this way. Leisure is the purest form of doing something for its own sake, but a partisan of vocation may argue that it would be difficult to separate the academic scientist from the leisured one. Both are motivated by and devoted to their activity and are so to the extent of valuing that work as an end. If the academic scientist would continue his activity even without the burden of necessity, the partisan of vocation argues, why should we hold leisure to be superior? However, there remains an important distinction underneath that surface overlap between vocation and leisure. While those with a vocation live for their work, the work itself has goals beyond it. In other words, the activity of vocation is rarely a final end in the Aristotelian sense. This is clear in a vocation like politics. The political actor that is primarily motivated by their cause ultimately desires a particular outcome to their work. The work itself is not the final end, it is instead their idea of justice. "Living for" requires going beyond remunerative motivations, but not to the full extent that Aristotelian leisure does. This is even true of Weber's scientist. Again, the scientist with a vocation has concerns beyond material reward, but the activity of science is not his final end but the progress of science.[12] There is a history and development to science, and it is the goal of science to be surpassed. Newton may have been a genius, but Einstein surpasses him. Though some antirealist philosophers of science may disagree, Weber holds that all science becomes and even "*cries out*" "to be surpassed and rendered obsolete."[13] It is not simply the fate of scientific work, but it is also its goal.

Weber recognizes that this inherent component of science becomes a threat to science as a vocation. Weber describes the threat in the form of asking the following incisive questions: "What meaningful achievement can he hope for from activities that are always doomed to obsolescence? What can justify his readiness to harness himself to this specialized, never-ending enterprise?"[14] Salvation is found in tempering and moderating romantic illusions about the nature of science. Only the religious and "overgrown children" believe in the power of science to either get closer to God or ascertain the "meaning" of the world.[15] In other words, Weber would have us deny the final end promised in Aristotelian leisure, arguing that his followers are "overgrown children." The logic of vocation, therefore, requires us to deny final ends. The scientist must fully face the necessarily progressive nature of his work. But, for Weber at least, this tempering is also a trueing. The tempering of expectations is a trueing of what it means to engage in science for its own sake. Weber follows Nietzsche in deriding the false optimism of the "overgrown children" that see the life of science "as the road to *happiness*."[16] We need to be careful of how far we take this side of Weber's critique, however. As a scholar himself, Weber is clearly alive to the promises of this way of life. The problem, as he understands it, is that naivety is both an intellectual error and also destructive to the personality of the scholar. The inevitable disappointment that will result will ruin any hope for science as a vocation. Science must be done for its own sake, but it needs to be tempered and trued by realistic and often disappointing expectations. Science does not result in the quiet and content contemplation of the meaning of the world, which was the intended goal of Aristotle's form of contemplation. As Weber's wife, Marianne, later recounted, when asked why he engaged in the life of the mind, Weber responded: "I want to see how much I can bear."[17]

Whereas Aristotle would describe scientific endeavor as the attempt to understand and appreciate truths of nature, the vocation of modern science, built on the same epistemological and moral foundations as liberalism, strives for itself to be made obsolete. If scientific activity did not seek to progress but only sought to understand the universe for the benefit of the scientist, science could not be publicly supported by a liberal regime. Modern science, therefore, also takes on the same cloak of the laborer: it seeks to be in continual motion and development. There are exceptions to this, one of which, art, is taken notice of by Weber. But as we will see later, it is precisely because it is an exception to this rule that art becomes problematic as a potential vocation.

Vocation is linked with leisure in another way. Just like leisure, not everyone is capable of it. And here, I do not mean the technical skill required of multifarious careers, though this too is required. Instead, I mean particular virtues of character. When speaking of the vocation of politics, Weber stands firm that not everyone is capable of undergoing a life of politics as a vocation: "An ethics of conviction and an ethics of responsibility are not absolute antitheses but are mutually complementary, and only when taken together do they constitute the authentic human being who *is capable* of having a 'vocation for politics.' "[18] It is the combining of the "ethics of conviction" and the "ethics of responsibility" that makes one capable of vocation. Though we can apply these seemingly opposing ethics to other vocations, Weber primarily discusses them within the context of politics. In the case of politics, the combining of these two ethics is the

54 | Leisure

uneasy blend of the intransigent idealist and the power-hungry political profiteer, both of which, when pursued on their own, without blending with the other, are problematic. Weber tells us that it is vanity that causes us to inappropriately follow one path or the other, but the results vary widely depending on which path is followed. The intransigent idealist is the more likely danger, and though Weber has some sympathy for this position, he has little patience with it. Weber, reasonably, connects an ethics of conviction with religious zeal.[19] This idealist does not care for the consequences of his actions, only with the justice of his principles. Though seemingly noble, Weber calls this archetype a "mere child" who does not understand that "it is *not* true that nothing but good comes from good and nothing but evil from evil, but rather quite frequently the opposite is the case. Anyone who does not realize this is in fact a mere child in political matters."[20] The childish idealist cannot understand, or refuses to out of self-righteousness, either the consequences of his actions or that occasionally acting against his principles will sometimes lead to a desired result. As in the case of the scientist who seeks to discover the secrets of the universe, Weber links all attempts at purity to childishness.

Not only do the principles of this childish idealist have their own dangers when taken too far, Weber doubts the sincerity of their strongest adherents: "I suspect that I should come to the conclusion that in nine cases out of ten I was dealing with windbags who do not genuinely feel what they are taking on themselves but who are making themselves drunk on romantic sensations."[21] The outward self-righteousness belies their supposed sincerity, and this is due to vanity. The zealot does not achieve enough distance from himself and becomes intoxicated by his own principles. Despite a concern for a principle, it is only the zealot himself that is served and aggrandized. He may not achieve power due to his stridency, but he retains the pleasure of feeling righteous. At its height, the ethics of conviction leads to the demagogue, who is concerned solely with the impression he makes and is not concerned enough for the outcome of his actions.[22]

The lack of distance from oneself is also responsible for the danger at the opposite pole. The politician who ascribes too much to the ethics of responsibility has a self-intoxication of another sort—an intoxication with power, regardless of the justice of outcomes. Whereas an ethics of conviction is the result of a vanity of passion, the ethics of responsibility is due to a vanity of the mind. The strict adherent of the former finds self-satisfaction in the righteousness of their principle, while, in the case

Vocation and the Radicalization of Labor | 55

of the latter, she finds it in her self-interested cleverness. This archetype strives for power for its own sake. Power is required in politics, and it sometimes finds those willing to serve at its altar without also serving at the altar of principle.

Weber often associates the ethics of conviction with an otherworldliness. Those acting from conviction often use religious language, and their motives are often, though not always, religious in nature. The ethics of responsibility, meanwhile, is associated with a concern for consequences in this world. It is utilitarian. Weber's views on religion are complicated, but in this context, he does not take issue with those concerned with the salvation of their souls. Though, as we will see, those with a political vocation need to combine the two, there is a characteristic danger to combining them in the wrong way. As Turner notes, there is a third category of value in Weber's system, and it involves attempting to use otherworldly values as a goal for this world.[23] In more familiar language, this is the attempt to create the kingdom of God on earth. Those insensitive to the ethic of responsibility mistake an impossibility for a practicable vision. Aside from not wishing to dirty oneself with compromise, those who mix otherworldly ends with this-worldly goals have a mistaken understanding of that which is achievable. Weber thought adherents to Christianity, and those who live in the wake of its dominance in the West, were particularly susceptible to making this mistake,[24] but it seems to be an all too human temptation.[25]

It is only through an abnegation of an aspect of the self, a rejection of vanity, that someone can achieve true selfhood in vocation, through this proper combination of conviction and responsibility, mediated by a "sense of proportion."[26] Some have argued that, for Weber, conviction and responsibility are mutually exclusive ethical systems.[27] However, though the possibility of such a combination may seem shaky, and indeed Weber does find it to be a treacherous line to walk, the two ethics are not, strictly speaking, exclusive. As Satkunanandan justly argues, Weber's responsibility does not mean extreme realism, but there is more room for morality in his system than is usually thought.[28] In fact, Weber goes so far as to call conviction and responsibility "mutually complementary."[29] The key to this position is, again, the issue of vanity. Without distance from oneself, our politician acting from conviction does not, truly, have conviction. Vanity corrupts conviction into self-righteousness, which keeps the politician from ever achieving anything in accordance with their supposed principles, saying, "The world is nasty, not I."[30] Those without responsibility and proportion to go along with conviction are therefore traitors to their own

56 | Leisure

principles. Refusing to use their reason alongside passion interrupts any possible welcome progress. Someone with true conviction, meanwhile, understands that good things sometimes come from the bad, and that bad consequences sometimes arise from good motives.

A political vocation requires this uneasy, but complementary, combination of conviction and responsibility. However, we should not limit such an analysis and prescription to political and scientific vocations. Though it is true that Weber thinks different vocations have somewhat different requirements—and this will be discussed in what follows—it remains that the requirements for a political vocation have import for vocation generally.[31] This is because the relationship between the two ethics represent the inherent tension between moral aspirations and various worldly necessities. Different vocations may have varyingly distinct challenges and corresponding methods of overcoming those challenges, but the overriding tension between the two, and the need to achieve a resolution between them, remains. For instance, in politics, vanity is the "deadly enemy."[32] Distance from oneself is the method of resolving conviction and responsibility. This is less true in the sciences: "in the case of the scholar, repugnant though it may be, [vanity] is relatively innocuous in the sense that as a rule it does not disrupt the business of scholarship."[33] Even more than being relatively innocuous, it is an "occupational disease." Vanity does not cause as much of a problem in academia but is near inherent to the psychology of the scholar.

Despite these differing dangers, the combination of conviction and responsibility remains necessary. Conviction in the sciences takes the form of passion and inspiration. Inspiration, Weber contends, is as necessary to the scientist as it is necessary to the artist.[34] Weber uses the same terminology of "intoxication" to describe the inspiration of the scientist as he does to sketch the conviction of the man with the political vocation.[35] The passion of Martin Luther King Jr., then, is inherently related to Plato's "mania." Inspiration is not wholly up to us, as it depends upon fate and natural talent that not all have.[36] But cultivation of passion and inspiration is also required in a vocation.

Personality and Vocation's Radicalization of Locke

Having a "personality," which requires inspiration and great devotion, is often synonymous with having a true vocation.[37] The two, personality and

Vocation and the Radicalization of Labor | 57

vocation, have similar characters and also the same origin in Protestant theology.[38] Like a vocation, a personality needs to be created and cultivated. We are not born with them. It was Protestant theology that created the concept and experience of personality, and, for the most part, only those who inherit that world are thereby capable of creating one.[39]

A personality, for Weber, is systematic unity of our inner lives. It is a tight coherence of our way of thinking and behaving in the world with our "ultimate values."[40] So far, this does not seem like a radical departure from many other possible comportments, and it is unclear why only those that inherit a Protestant worldview would be capable of personality. A coherence between our values and our way of thinking and acting has a basic name that finds form in seemingly all cultures—we call it "integrity." The key difference is that the "ultimate values" are chosen by the individual. It is not enough that we have ultimate values and that we act and think in line with those values. We must also make a conscious choice between possible values. Those with true personalities need to be free of external influences, *including those of nature*. According to Weber, nature cannot be the source of ultimate values, and it must not be understood to be such by those with a personality. Having a personality, while ultimately an extension of the self, involves a form of self-denial—a denial of natural impulses.[41]

Going beyond personality's relation with the specific vocation of the scholar, it is worth noting that Weber's conception of personality is much like Locke's self-authorship. Both require radical self-control and responsibility. Both also understand this self-control and responsibility to be against nature. This is clearest in Weber, but we see it in Locke as well. For Locke, nature furnishes us with the goal of felicity but does not furnish us with the means of acquiring it. That is wholly up to us, and we must reject and overcome nature to achieve it.

Furthermore, Locke's calling and Weber's vocation both require an education and cultivation. As we saw, the entirety of Locke's education is aimed at the preparation for a calling, and such a calling requires particular virtues of character. Even if the means of achieving such a state often require a paternalistic guide, the end goal is rational self-control.[42] A calling also requires intellectual virtues, as someone who requires a calling needs to understand, and appreciate, the utilitarian calculus often involved in choosing an immediate unease with a later, and greater, release from unease. These virtues are not exhaustive but representative of the kinds of characteristics required of those training for a calling.

58 | Leisure

Though particular virtues such as rational self-control are not often written about explicitly by Weber, they are very much implied. Shaping a personality, for example, requires a constancy of our inner lives with our ultimate values. And as we saw, this requires self-denial of a kind. It is a denial of many of our natural drives and impulses in order to aim at goals that are likewise not demanded of us by nature but are imposed on us by our very selves. This creation of the personality, because it involves the choice of values and the rational direction of one's interior life in line with those values, necessarily includes great self-control. Though Weber does not mention or include Locke in his analysis, we can say that Locke represents the secularization of the Protestant moral ideal that Weber thought was beginning to reign in Europe.[43]

There are important ways vocation goes beyond, and radicalizes, Lockean labor, however. Most importantly, though both conceptions focus on the need for self-direction and creation, they are to different ends. Weber denies the possibility of reasoning between ultimate values. What is important is self-creation, so long as it operates with an eye to conviction, responsibility, and proportion. This position is worked out in Weber's discussion of science as a vocation:

> The assumption that I am offering you here is based on a fundamental fact. This is that as long as life is left to itself and is understood in its own terms, it knows only that the conflict between these gods is never-ending. Or, in nonfigurative language, life is about the incompatibility of ultimate *possible* attitudes and hence the inability ever to resolve the conflicts between them. Hence the necessity of *deciding* between them. Whether in these circumstances it is worth anyone's while to choose science as a "vocation" and whether science itself has an objectively worthwhile "vocation" is itself a value judgment about which nothing useful can be said in the lecture room. This is because positively affirming the value of science is the *precondition* of all teaching.[44]

Both Weber and Locke require choice. Weber requires us to choose a particular vocation over another. Locke also requires choice throughout his ethical and epistemological writings. However, Locke would be unlikely to call Weber's "decision" an actual choice, as Weber is pessimistic about a rational resolution to "deciding" between ultimate values. While Locke requires choice and self-creation, he still holds on to the possibility and promise of rational resolution. He believes a complete and fully demonstrable ethical system is possible, for instance. Also, as we saw, he requires that we ourselves reach rational conclusions about the external world. We need to think through and demonstrate these conclusions ourselves for them to be considered knowledge, but it is still knowledge, not an arbitrary choice between possible conclusions. For Weber, those of us that inherit the rationalized and demystified world created in large part by Protestantism must choose a vocation, and choose it for its own sake, in order to create meaning in our lives, but there is no ultimate justification of whether such dedication to that particular vocation is warranted. We can use "reason" if we wish, but reason is, in the end, unfit for the task.

Despite this important disagreement, Weber's account of vocation remains a coherent and otherwise consistent working out of Locke's notions of labor and a calling. The hope Weber has for vocation is that it will create meaning in an increasingly demystified and potentially meaningless world. As such, he requires that vocation be weighty and done for its own sake. This also means that it cannot simply be understood in terms of moneymaking. Vocations, in the modern world, must support us materially, but this cannot be their only, or even primary, role. Thus, he takes issue with Benjamin Franklin, and his influence, in *The Protestant Ethic and the Spirit of Capitalism*.[45] There is a danger now that the religious foundations underlying the value of a calling have, for the most part, washed away. Money and wealth can be served as ends, which Weber, understandably, finds to be inadequate. As we saw in the last chapter, Locke also understands labor, work, and the calling to be valuable beyond their material utility. They of course also serve those ends, but they have a crucial importance besides. In this way, we cannot understand Locke's attachment to labor to be simply a part of some "possessive individualism" that serves enrichment over all else. Furthermore, though Locke's relationship with religion is complicated and full of controversy, Locke provides a justification for labor that does not require the inclusion of God or the afterlife.

So, there is a coherence between Locke and Weber here, but Weber develops the notion further by describing the psychological state of those actually attached to vocation. Locke tells us something of the promise and necessity of labor and a calling, but Weber develops more completely the inner desires and, also, the possible challenges of those that dedicate their lives to a vocation, especially in light of the secularization of the West.

60 | Leisure

Vocation: Synthesis of Leisure and Labor?

As a development of Lockean labor, vocation's relation to leisure is similar to that of Locke's. It is primarily an inversion of the values of leisure. However, there are important nuances to be explored. For instance, in radicalizing labor, vocation comes closer to leisure than labor in some areas, especially in understanding its activity more fully as an end. By extending beyond labor, it occasionally circles around to leisure. It is therefore tempting to say that vocation could be an incorporation of leisure into work. Today, work is less likely to be the toil that Aristotle found to be corrupting of the body and soul. We now get to choose an activity for ourselves, and this seems to take us beyond the realm of necessity, and into the realm of freedom, just like leisure. Still, despite this temptation to see an overlap between these two ways of life, vocation remains a competitor to leisure, with its focus on self-creation through activity that is progressive and constantly overcomes itself.

The overlap between leisure and vocation is also superficially present in that both are achieved, and these kinds of achievement are related. As argued in chapter 1, leisure is not simply the absence of work or other responsibility but itself requires virtues. Vocation demands similar virtues. For instance, the moderation required to push away the useful in favor of the useless in leisure is much the same as the need to combine conviction and responsibility in a vocation. Weber's "power politician" does not properly have a vocation without a settled conviction. That critique is similar to one of Aristotle's critiques of the Spartans. The Spartans, who certainly have elements of moderation and courage, only have those virtues for the end of military success. Likewise, Weber's power politician seeks power for its own sake and is not guided by conviction. Aristotle and Weber certainly use different language, but the problems and proposed solutions overlap. Vocation is not, and cannot be, pure career success. Translating such an analysis to a language more characteristic of Aristotle, the power politician is obsessed with the means to the point of neglecting the ends. Mistaking the means as an end is both a moral and intellectual error. Whereas Weber would call it a failed resolution of conviction and responsibility, Aristotle would deem it an intellectual failure that demonstrates a lack of true moral virtue, since the excellences of character are not aimed at the proper target.

As both are forms of achievement, there arises another potential source of overlap between leisure and vocation: they are both aristocratic, a feature of vocation noticed and critiqued by some of the more

Vocation and the Radicalization of Labor | 61

astute opponents of modernity, such as Zygmunt Bauman.[46] It is partly so because it is exclusive—many, if not most, are kept from participating simply by the class into which they are born. However, more importantly, it is aristocratic in the sense that leisure is an achievement and not given to someone based on natural dignity.

Vocation is not aristocratic in the political sense. The very concept and experience of vocation is a modern development, and it has arisen alongside the loosening and eventual destruction of claims of birthright. In other words, virtually everyone in a liberal society has the opportunity to pursue vocation. Certainly, there may be unequal access to education and other goods that improve the chances of achieving some vocations, but there are no formal barriers stipulating that those born into one class become, say, millworkers, while those of another class become, say, physicians. So, it is not aristocratic in the way Nietzsche describes older forms of nobility. The greatness of someone with a vocation does not stem from an inherent and internal beauty and goodness. Vocation is a way of being, but it is one that is shaped and created—it is not a quality with which someone is born. Vocation as a way of life must be *wrested* from our natural state. For the Protestant theologians that created vocation, our natural being is sinful and must be overcome. Our being may become noble and worthy but, unlike old forms of nobility, it does not find its goodness inherent and natural to itself.[47]

Vocation, therefore, has the democratic component of there being no birthright or inherent goodness associated with one class over another. Despite being democratic in this way, however, vocation is elitist in the sense that one must become worthy of a vocation. Regardless of particular path chosen, some virtues or characteristics, such as self-control, instrumental rationality, and the combination of conviction and responsibility are required. Beyond these, individual vocations will have their own forms of education that combine technical skill and, likely, character virtues. Being a nurse, for instance, requires much more than technical skills such as placing an IV. And those character virtues may be more demanding than the technical ones.[48] This is why someone like Weber, who found much to praise in vocation and prescribed it as a way of creating meaning in a world that was quickly becoming demystified, also thought vocation would be an impressive accomplishment. We all want a vocation—we even feel that we need one[49]—but it is still an accomplishment, and a difficult one.

Both leisure and vocation make claims to being valuable ways of life, but though there is some notable overlap in those ways of life, we must now emphasize how they remain radically different. Both leisure

62 | Leisure

and vocation are both understood as being done for their own sakes. However, there are different usages at work. In vocation, the "for its own sake" is meant psychologically. When we say that a doctor works for work's sake, we mean that that is how she understands her motivations and also her identity. It is not simply for the material reward, but she understands her work as being valuable, not just to others but also to herself, in a way that transcends a material utility calculus. We remain agnostic, however, about whether being a doctor is actually worthy of such devotion. What is important to our, and Weber's, understanding of vocation, is the psychological motivation and self-understanding of the work. We may have some hazily defined limit as to what is and is not acceptable as a vocation, but the range is wide—nearly infinitely so. Not only does the doctor have a vocation, but so does the banker. Even the water-skier that turns professional could claim to have a vocation, and Weber would not seem to have any grounds for denying such a claim. If Weber denies that the water-skier has a vocation, it is merely, as Strauss occasionally said of Weber, a noble example of Weber not following through with his principles.[50]

Aristotle, too, understands leisure as an end in itself, but the interior understanding and devotion is insufficient, or even distinctive of true leisure. It is not enough that the doctor understands herself as doing her work for its own sake—it needs to be worthy of such devotion. As we saw, Weber thinks there are virtues and qualities of character that are required in order to have a vocation. Cultivating and maintaining meaning in our work requires virtue. However, Aristotle may reply that such virtues are meaningless or valueless unless channeled in specific directions.

Moving beyond Vocation

The radicalization of Locke found in contemporary vocation has a number of benefits, including the explicit emphasis upon choosing an activity for its own sake, even if the "for its own sake" is not as demanding as Aristotle's, or at least demanding in different ways. The benefit of this is that it opens the door to deriving a great source of meaning from careers,[51] whereas previous conceptions of work saw it as a necessary evil. What a great development it would be, then, if vocations were able to provide us with needs and comforts of both the body and soul. However, vocation has not fulfilled its ambition, or at least it has fulfilled it insufficiently. In

Vocation and the Radicalization of Labor | 63

what follows, I sketch why this is the case, and why, given its own logic, vocation was never likely to succeed. In such an analysis, we also begin to see what it may mean for a future that goes beyond vocation.

The first problem stems from the aforementioned issue of choice. Cultivating such characteristics is not easy, but rational control of oneself in the service of an eventual calling is, for Locke, the explicit purpose of education (*Thoughts* §201). The concern here is: Self-control in the service of what? Since Locke and Weber refuse to definitively argue that one vocation can be better than another, we are left with the possibility that the professional water-skier has as much of a vocation as the public servant. Aristotle's education at least has the virtue of limiting the range of worthy activity and prescribing certain ways of life over others. Without such an education, Aristotle may argue that we will end up with more water-skiers than public servants. To some extent, this criticism is unfair—it places a standard upon Locke and Weber that they themselves did not choose. Weber would argue that there is no ground to judge one vocation over another. Unless we can demonstrate that such ground exists, the criticism is moot.

The second problem with vocation is its combination of means and ends. If the combination proves to be impossible or insupportably difficult, vocation becomes untenable, as this combination of means and ends is part of its nature and its promise. Vocation, and useful activity generally, is praised by Locke for two reasons: First, it is the practice of rationality and thereby a component of self-authorship. Second, it is praised for its distracting qualities. However, its promise also becomes its downfall. We expect vocation to supply us with the means of our material existence, while also becoming a central source of meaning. The problem is, even for those whose vocational activity could genuinely become a source of meaning, that meaning is threatened by its mixing with the material means of existence. Though Marx and his followers rightfully point to alienation as a source of disappointment with capitalist labor, the problem here is even simpler: the charm of an activity is often ruined by being rewarded for it. In a famous study, Lepper and colleagues demonstrate that external motivations not only work differently than internal motivations, but that the external *erode* internal motivations.[52] In the case of vocation, an otherwise meaningful activity loses its value when we are paid for it.

There is, no doubt, a satisfaction in being paid for our labor, and using that payment to take charge of our life. However, that satisfaction is distinct from, and inherently dangerous to, the satisfaction derived from

64 | Leisure

the work itself. This point is recognized by nonliberal partisans of labor, such as the agrarian writer Wendell Berry. In his novel *Hannah Coulter*, the harshest criticism of another's work is likening them to a "damned employee."[53] The contrast is between a paid employee who only cares for the result of her labor, rather than the work of a "member" of the community. These "members" often own their own land, but not always, and the work they do is not always on their own farms. At harvest, for instance, the members share each other's labor as needed. While the products will eventually be sold at market, this relation to labor is profoundly different from the work of those with a bourgeois vocation. Because of the demand to be self-authors, contemporary vocation is, at bottom, individualistic, rather than the communal work portrayed by Berry, where good work is the product of bonds with a community, not individual economic incentive. Without such bonds, which they must necessarily be without, those striving for vocation become "damned employees." Payment becomes the final end and thereby corrupts the work itself. I will not go so far as to say that it is impossible to satisfactorily combine means and ends in a vocation, but that it is a rare achievement. Alone, this elitist nature of vocation is not necessarily problematic, but the democratic origins of vocations sit ill at ease with this elitism, and it becomes increasingly distasteful and unsatisfying for those that attempt, and fail, to have a vocation.[54]

Intertwined with the second, the third problem with vocation is the illusory nature of the choice involved in vocation. Vocation radicalizes Locke by transforming work from a rational and industrious self-creation, primarily in the form of material responsibility, to a self-discovery and expression that seeks to align action with ultimate values that cannot themselves be rationally chosen. But vocation retains the economic responsibility component of Lockean labor, requiring each of us to find both moral and material sustenance in our work. This may seem to be a welcome moderation of Locke's demand to be industrious: moral and political concerns place a limit on our industriousness, or at least give that industriousness a rosy form. But what seems to be a moderation is another coherent development and radicalization. Rather than limit economic industriousness, we have made moral and political action economic and industrious. We cannot afford to devote ourselves to a cause; we must be paid for that work. Even more, this becomes another way vocation fails itself: its incorporation of economic necessity means that our vocation becomes subservient to that economic necessity, and few will be able to shape legitimate vocations within a capitalist economic order. Said more

Vocation and the Radicalization of Labor | 65

plainly, aside from the rarity of the virtues needed for vocation, economic demand limits the number of openings in meaningful careers. As de Botton claims, in agreement with psychological research on the subject, jobs feel meaningful when we "generate delight or reduce suffering in others."[55] Even if we expand this to those who view their work as an end, such as scholars and artists, it would be difficult to honestly conclude that those with a "meaningful" career form anything close to a half of the working adult population of the United States.

Allow me a personal anecdote to illustrate. While waiting for my cell phone to be repaired in a local phone repair shop, I began chatting with an employee. He asked me what I did for a living, and I told him that I taught politics and philosophy at the local college. He responded by saying that he wanted to major in philosophy when he was in college, but there was only one job to get by following such a path, and that was to be a philosophy professor. He then enthusiastically congratulated me on attaining that one job for philosophy majors. Of course, not all philosophy majors become professors, and there is substantial evidence of those in the humanities going on to have successful careers in a wide variety of areas.[56] However, while the man repairing my phone was wrong in that sense, he was homing in on a more important truth: philosophy majors want to do philosophy, but a philosophy professor is the only career path for those with that interest and bearing. But the market, obviously, cannot support everyone becoming a philosophy professor, even those who major in the subject. And sadly, only a fraction who complete doctoral studies, even when admissions to those programs are themselves incredibly competitive, ever attain significant employment as college faculty. The market requires many more to repair cell phones than to study and teach philosophy.

Philosophy is an extreme example, but how many have the opportunity to do work they consider as an end, or that helps others in a more substantial way than selling goods and services? Even if Locke is right that labor, in the form of repairing cell phones, does not have to be corrupting, vocation promises much more than a lack of corruption—it promises happiness. Let us not sink to the absurdity that the repairing of cell phones could be understood by many to be a vocation. Even ignoring the probability that many vocations are corrupted by being shaped by economic constraints, having these vocations is not just an accomplishment, it is a privilege. Even if capable, many, if not most, are left out of the experience of vocation. Vocation promises the shaping of the self and the world. It promises that personality can defeat fortune.

66 | Leisure

This is its claim over aristocratic leisure. Vocation is open for everyone to give it a go. But many who give it a serious attempt, and also develop the virtues to succeed, still fail. Therefore, vocation has insufficiently reshaped the world for talent over fortune. Fortune remains, only hidden, which only heightens the pain of fortune. Those in an aristocracy can resign themselves to their plight, but those who fail at vocation are left either blaming themselves, perhaps unjustly, for their failure or, even worse, are left forever wondering at the cause of their failure, whether it was a failure of talent, or a failure of fortune.

Conclusion

Weber's conception of a vocation remains the contemporary vision, as we see in contemporary vocation self-help books. One of the more notable, and serious, examples of this is Parker Palmer's *Let Your Life Speak: Listening for the Voice of Vocation*. The title of the book is telling. The focus of vocation moves from the rational self-authorship of Locke and transforms into a self-discovery. Vocation is less about *making* yourself into something as *listening* to what your self wants you to be.[57] Addressing the position of Locke, consciously or not, Palmer critiques his earlier self that wished to impose an outside logic, which he calls an act of violence:

> Vocation, the way I was seeking it, becomes an act of will, a grim determination that one's life will go this way or that whether it wants to or not . . . the willful pursuit of vocation is an act of violence toward ourselves—violence in the name of a vision that, however lofty, is forced on the self from without rather than grown from within. True self, when violated, will always resist us, sometimes at great cost, holding our lives in check until we honor its truth.[58]

What Palmer calls "willfulness," Locke would call freedom—freedom of holding yourself accountable to a rationally created law. Palmer argues that this is violence against the true self, and even if such laws are noble, the self will always rebel. A vocation cannot come from outside of us. We must, therefore, listen to what the self wants, not impose upon it with violence. This is true of even the irrational elements of our soul: our task, for Palmer and for other partisans of vocation, is to also "listen" to what is "shameful" in us.[59]

Vocation and the Radicalization of Labor | 67

While there is a critique of Lockean liberty here, it is also a direct descendant of it. There is a reason why Palmer was attracted to that self-creation in his early life. His transformation is not a massive revolution from his earlier position, but a play upon it. Of course, realizing the self is not an easy task. Finding one's calling remains a great challenge, one that Palmer undergoes and narrates in impressive depth. Palmer suggests searching for a "true self" that exists behind a mask of "self-serving fictions."[60] These self-serving fictions should remind us of what Weber calls vanity. The political worker that is vain is likely to be overly beholden to principles. These principles tend to be self-serving: by refusing to compromise, we show ourselves to be self-righteous. Palmer intends something broader here, but he shares with Weber the idea that vanity is the enemy of true vocation.

It is in the realizing of the self that freedom is found. Part of the challenge of vocation is recognizing our individual limitations. While this may seem to be a lack of freedom, as it denies us unlimited options, there is a greater freedom found in accepting those limitations: "each time a door closes, the rest of the world opens up."[61] The logic is something like the following. Keeping all of our options open is a form of freedom, but we need to start down a path for the real choices to appear. In the realm of vocation, it is only once we listen to ourselves, and begin following ourselves, that we begin to explore our true depth. Having that initial choice is a necessary prerequisite, but we have to get over that initial hump to fully develop and recognize the richness of our own selves.

I think there is reason to be concerned about vocation as an ideal. As Weber makes clear, and Palmer glosses over, vocation denies itself. There is no objective reason to pick one vocation over the other. Palmer's vocation, he tells us, involves serving others.[62] However, there is no reason why that needs to be ours. There is nothing internal to vocation that keeps us from *stealing* from others as our vocation. Even further, there is no reason to choose vocation in the first place. If we merely need to choose, why choose to find the self in work? Why not choose it in leisure? Vocation takes the logic of work and labor to the furthest extreme and, in so doing, pulls up its own foundations. I think this was always going to lead to dissatisfaction, and in this dissatisfaction we open the door to leisure.

The disappointment with vocation is neither universal nor complete. Surely, some do find meaning in their careers and are able to successfully navigate the fraught combination of means and ends. The claim here, instead, is that the disappointment of vocation has reached, or is reaching, a tipping point. However, not only is the disappointment not universal,

68 | Leisure

it is also not with every aspect of vocation. Even if we are dissatisfied in the failure of vocation to achieve its goals, this does not mean we are necessarily dissatisfied with the goals themselves. Its goals are both broad and specific. The broadness comes from its claim to happiness, through the specific goals of self-creation, expression, and "meaningfulness." The cynicism regarding vocation has not made us return freshly to the question of happiness. Instead, we are holding on to self-creation and meaningful activity and beginning to deny the central role of marketized work in that self-creation and meaningful activity. Evidence of this is seen in two phenomena: the increase in contemporary "critiques" of work in favor of greater "leisure," and the increase in job dissatisfaction and the resulting increase in idling at work.[63] These developments demonstrate, I think, less a desire for leisure than a desire for meaningful activity. But a desire for meaningful activity cannot supply its accomplishment, and vocation was never going to achieve meaningful activity for most. Contemporary analysis on potential leisure remains less about leisure, or even a critique of work, so much as an expression of a wish that work was more meaningful. And never, or rarely, questioned is the goal of happiness through self-creation, only the beginning realization that market labor is not succeeding.

It is on the basis of this very particular disappointment with work, then, that we will consider our current and potential future with leisure. Our understanding of self-authorship will alter in this transformation, but it will not be left behind. It is Rousseau who offers a critique of liberalism, from the very concern for individuality, and provides an ode to, and defense of, idleness. I have suggested that the logic underneath vocation could just as easily lead to leisure, and we will turn to an example of that very logic in Rousseau's example of idleness.

Chapter 4

Rousseau's Harmless and Happy Idleness

Introduction

The primary model of leisure we have seen thus far has been that of Aristotle. We have also seen the liberal rejection of that model in favor of rational industry. We cannot have both. We cannot have a substantive leisure supported by a regime while also understanding freedom as rational self-authorship that fully flowers in the industrious creation of wealth. On Locke's account, "leisure" is merely an irrational giving over to simple pleasures that corrupt and make us unhappy. But this is not the end of the story of leisure, as the understanding of freedom as rational industriousness, while still with us to some degree, has also developed into freedom as the self-discovery and expression that we see in the desire and search for vocation. In adapting to this new model of freedom, the door to leisure has been reopened. Rousseau's "leisure," what we typically translate as "idleness," adopts just such an account of freedom, as primarily and beautifully explored in his *Reveries of the Solitary Walker*.[1]

Reading Rousseau's *Reveries* accomplishes two things. First, it models a leisure that does not require political revolution. Achieving Aristotle's model of leisure would require a fundamental reshaping of politics, and we would not accept much of what would be instituted in such a regime. Aristotle requires the rejection of freedom to choose the ultimate good— and also requires slavery to support the leisure of citizens. Meanwhile, Rousseau wrote of, and lived, a leisure without revolution. Aside from allowing us to imagine a leisure without slavery, it also presents a leisure

70 | Leisure

that coexists alongside an industrious and, therefore, unleisured world. Second, and more important, reading Rousseau allows us to see leisure that is consistent with freedom as following inclination. As it turns out, becoming idle on this model is surprisingly difficult. Still, Rousseau claims he is happiest while idle, and the nature of this happiness and this idleness will be our next subject.

Aside from the account of idleness and its relationship to happiness, interrogating Rousseau's *Reveries* clarifies Rousseau's concern for nature and freedom. As Schwartz argues, human nature and human freedom, as well as their relation, "are always Rousseau's central questions."[2] Beginning with nature, I argue that Rousseau's idleness is not so much a return to nature as a transcendence beyond, but consistent with, nature. Though it is true that Rousseau's "savage" of the *Second Discourse* is also idle, Rousseau's personal idleness, and likewise any idleness we could hope for, remains distinct from uncivilized idleness. We have been changed too much by civilization, which required the development of faculties that were dormant in the state of nature. The composition of our idleness must therefore be different. Rousseau becomes an amateur botanist, for instance, a hobby not possible before the development of complex speech. Idleness is not to be understood as a lack of activity but a lack of duty, obligation, and external reward. Further, Rousseau's development allows him to experience greater happiness, as seen in his experience of the sentiment of existence, the "expansion of being," and in his use of imagination. However, what connects "civilized" idleness to uncivilized idleness is the reconstruction of natural goodness, especially in the form of freedom from vanity.

At the same time that idleness demands freedom from vanity, idleness is also the ground of achieving our natural freedom. The freedom of idleness is different from, and even opposed to, the freedom of the citizen, but idleness is how we concretely connect to freedom as inclination and will, rather than freedom as the fulfillment of obligation and duty. We should already recognize, then, that examining Rousseau on idleness is not a mere academic endeavor. If we wish for idleness today, Rousseau demands we overcome both vanity and duty, both of which, according to Rousseau, are inherent to civilization. Rousseau's challenge is therefore, at least partly, our own: How do we achieve idleness in a world that demands we not be so? What is promised in that idleness? And is such an achievement normatively defensible?

Solitude

Rousseau's idleness is of a particular kind, and his idleness necessitates a particular form of solitude as well. The particularity and the necessity of Rousseau's solitude will thereby be our first clue to Rousseau's idleness. Let us begin at the middle, with the most famous scene of the *Reveries*. There, in the Fifth Walk, Rousseau movingly describes his life's happiest moments:[3]

> I would slip away and go throw myself alone into a boat that I rowed to the middle of the lake when the water was calm; and there, stretching myself out full-length in the boat, my eyes turned to heaven, I let myself slowly drift back and forth with the water, sometimes for several hours, plunged in a thousand confused, but delightful, reveries which, even without having any well-determined or constant object, were in my opinion a hundred times preferable to the sweetest things I had found in what are called the pleasures of life.[4]

Not only does Rousseau describe what he was doing during this peak point of his life, he also describes the nature of the happiness that he experienced:

> What do we enjoy in such a situation? Nothing external to ourselves, nothing if not ourselves and our own existence. As long as this state lasts, we are sufficient unto ourselves, like God. The sentiment of existence, stripped of any other emotion, is in itself a precious sentiment of contentment and of peace which alone would suffice to make this existence dear and sweet to anyone able to spurn all the sensual and earthly impressions which incessantly come to distract us from it and to trouble its sweetness here-below.[5]

Consider first the circumstances surrounding Rousseau's float: it is a form of escape from others. He enjoys the company of those on the island, but when the pause for lunch "took too long and good weather beckoned,"[6] he would make his escape. Rousseau even rows to the center of the lake, which is the furthest point from human civilization. Not only is Rousseau alone here, he also actively *leaves* the company of others and gets as far from them as possible.

While drifting, he finds himself "plunged in a thousand confused, but delightful, reveries."[7] And when the lake is too rough for peaceful drifting, Rousseau sits on a secluded piece of the shore and sinks into a reverie that makes him "feel [his] existence with pleasure."[8] Rousseau must escape others because it is alone that we fully feel the sentiment of existence. He does not feel the sentiment of existence, in these peak moments, in communion or in solidarity with others. To fully feel his being is to feel it in its natural state—which is alone. Rousseau does not say that his reverie led to *our* experience of our *shared* existence but *my* feeling of *my* existence.[9] Others, therefore, could only distract and detract from this experience of enjoying "nothing external to ourselves."[10] Rousseau does raise the possibility of experiencing the sentiment of existence as a "sociable man," but this is a weakened and almost always corrupted experience because it requires the judgment and opinions of others.[11] Aside from the greater potential for that sentiment being corrupt, it is also less intense, as it is always indirect and must always involve beings external to ourselves. The happiness found in idleness is not the same as the happiness of the citizen, and they may even contradict one another, but they are both manifestations of the psychic unity necessary of human happiness in all its forms.[12] Most civilized humans are divided against themselves, but the peak of civilian life is found in the wholeness of the social body and common unity.[13] However, the unity of the idler is more proximate to our original unity, which demands a lack of obligation, as we will see.

As made clear in the *Second Discourse*, the sentiment of existence was our first sentiment, existing prior to civilization.[14] To experience it, then, is a way of reaching back to our original condition. Marks argues that the sentiment of existence is not ingrained in us,[15] but I find this argument to be a stretch, especially given clear contrary statements in the *Second Discourse*, such as: "Man's first sentiment was that of his existence."[16] Whether an infant feels his existence is beside the point, as even Rousseau will count as natural those faculties and abilities that we necessarily develop. However, Marks's overriding point, which I do find to be persuasive, is that the enjoyment of the sentiment of existence, at least to the extent that Rousseau does, is something beyond the capabilities of original man.[17] This is what is intended by describing Rousseau's brand of idleness as a transcendence, rather than a return to nature. Rousseau transcends the "savage," while remaining coherent with the principles of nature, and avoiding the corruptions of society. The savage may not be miserable like most civilized persons, but Rousseau goes beyond the capacities of the savage to achieve a higher happiness. As will be elaborated later, this is also accomplished in the use of the imagination and in the "expansion of being."

Though Rousseau's rowing to the center of Lake Bienne, and his meditation aside it, are repeated activities on St. Peter's Island, his founding of a rabbit colony is a single act. In this strange and short scene, Rousseau describes himself as a founder, and it is here that we see Rousseau's most social act on the island. However, even here, we see that it remains more solitary than not. First, Rousseau is only founding a society, not joining one—he leaves the smaller island after releasing the rabbits. The conditions on the smaller island are perfect for the rabbits,[18] which not only speaks to Rousseau's general pessimism about the chances of founding just and happy regimes[19] but is even more important in its relation to his solitude. Rousseau would not have been interested in this beneficent act if further responsibilities were placed upon him as a result of his founding. After the releasing of the rabbits, it is up to forces outside of himself as to whether they are strong enough to survive the winter.[20] He gives them the best chances to survive and thrive but washes his hands of the ultimate outcome. This helps demonstrate that it is not simply the presence of or interaction with others that Rousseau dislikes about society, but it is the bounding of his freedom, found in duty and obligation, that is offensive to Rousseau. As he states in his first letter to Malesherbes, his lazy independence is responsible for the "slightest duties of civil life" being unbearable.[21] Grant is correct to note that social relationships that do not admit of vanity are possible,[22] and dependence is not itself necessarily to be avoided,[23] but such relationships are rare and difficult, and solitude is Rousseau's method of retaining his natural goodness.

We also see his hesitancy with duty in his rejection of charity in the Sixth Walk. Rousseau took great pleasure in helping a disabled boy, but: "This pleasure, having gradually become a habit, was inexplicably transformed into a kind of duty I soon felt to be annoying, especially because of the preliminary harangue to which I had to listen and in which he never failed to call me Monsieur Rousseau many times, to show that he knew me."[24] Rousseau's paranoia comes into play here, but even that is not the primary issue. The primary problem is that the single act of charity transformed into a duty, which undermines his need to follow his own inclination. Continuing to give charity would be done, not because

74 | Leisure

of an in-the-moment feeling of pity, but because of an obligation, which is necessarily at odds with independence understood as passionately following one's inclination.[25] The isolated act of charity, free from duty, is beautiful in much the same way as the isolated reverie is beautiful. Once duty is added, the charm is lost.[26]

Rousseau is able to follow his inclination in founding the rabbit colony without having later duties. It is for this reason that Rousseau needs to tell us that founding the colony was his own idea.[27] His motivation seemingly comes from a similar place as his desire to help the disabled boy. Rousseau, then, is not strictly alone, but his relations with others lack obligation. As Lane argues, Rousseau keeps "emotional distance" from others on the island.[28] This is reflective of solitude in the state of nature, but more importantly this form of solitude is necessary to his idleness, which is also reflective of natural idleness. Social idleness would not allow him to experience the peak pleasures of the sentiment of existence, and, as we will see later, this will also become Rousseau's central justification for his idleness being morally defensible.

Calming of Reason

Not only are Rousseau's "thousand" reveries marked by solitude, they are also absent of coherent connection. They are "confused . . . without having any well-determined or constant object."[29] Later along the shore, he notes that he feels and enjoys the sentiment of his existence "without taking the trouble to think."[30] There are several stated reasons for the lack of coherent thought found in Rousseau's reveries: his intellectual powers have waned, he does not derive much satisfaction from the activity, and the results of such thinking would no longer be of benefit to him. However, there is a greater issue underlying or overriding each of those explanations: the human being is not by nature rational.[31] Rousseau is certainly not in the state of nature while on St. Peter's Island. For instance, he is there with others, and he interacts with and enjoys their company daily. However, nature again is his compass, especially during his moments of reverie. Whereas Aristotle, perhaps the only philosopher who privileges leisure and idleness as much or more than Rousseau in the *Reveries*, finds theoretical contemplation to be the peak of leisure,[32] Rousseau seeks to go beneath, and also transcend, theoretical contemplation in his idleness. He goes beneath by pointing to primordial man who does not have the ability to reason. However, this is also a transcendence. Being exposed to civilization, Rousseau must *overcome* the tendency to reason. Being a sentiment, the sentiment of existence cannot be achieved by reason. Rousseau would occasionally feel thoughts and ideas arising in him during his reveries, but he would push them aside.[33] Just as Rousseau must push aside the company of others to achieve the sentiment of existence, he must also do the same with theoretical contemplation. Rather than joining Aristotle in carefully separating leisure from other inferior forms of idleness, like play,[34] Rousseau elevates idleness above leisure or even in denying any difference between the two.[35]

The difference between Aristotle and Rousseau on this question stems from their disagreement over human nature, and this difference goes far in explaining Rousseau's insistence on the calming and shaping of reason. Whereas Aristotle finds the development of reason to be a development and fulfillment of our nature, Rousseau denies the necessity of reason, instead arguing that freedom is what separates us from other beings.[36] Masters is correct that Rousseau's emphasis on freedom is what separates him most from classical political philosophy.[37] However, Rousseau is not alone in this emphasis, and we therefore need to be more precise and separate him from the other moderns that also emphasize freedom. The separation of these two, reason and freedom, is perhaps what most makes Rousseau unique among the moderns. He agrees with Hobbes and Locke that freedom marks our natural condition, but Rousseau is singular in driving a wedge between freedom and reason. Locke also finds us to be free agents, but reason is part of freedom and he separates it from irrational license.[38] Whereas for Locke, the will must be combined with reason in order to achieve freedom, Rousseau separates those faculties, allowing us to be free without reason. Instead of having its source in reason, Rousseau's will has its source in the sentiment of existence.[39] The irrational might be unfree for Locke, whereas the will *precedes* reason for Rousseau. Our will need not be reasonable, we must only be conscious of it, in the same way that we are conscious of our own existence.

Given the emphasis on the lack of certain forms of rationality, Rousseau's interest in botany should surprise us. Botany involves investigation and, importantly, classification. This seeming paradox, however, helps us further clarify Rousseau's transcendence beyond our natural condition. Notice first that Rousseau is careful to separate his interest in botany from the typical way in which the subject is studied. When describing his love of botany in greater detail in the Seventh Walk, Rousseau mentions that

76 | Leisure

it is "without profit" and "without progress."[40] In seeking to understand the plants around him, Rousseau is not hoping to find nutritious plants or those that have medicinal qualities.[41] Such a concern would not be enjoyable and would undermine Rousseau's pastoral pleasures: "I even feel that the pleasure I take in wandering through groves would be poisoned by the sentiment of human infirmities, if I were led to think about fever, stones, gout, or epilepsy."[42] There are two motivations for such a statement. First, there is the psychological fact that undergoing an activity for some other sake undermines the pleasure we derive from it. And second, this comment also seems to be motivated by the deeper concern with living consistent with nature. Though the study of plants may not seem natural given Rousseau's portrayal of the faculty of understanding as unnatural, this is even more the case when it comes to studying plants for their utility. Rousseau's enjoyment is a simple delight in curiosity. He does not seek to write books so as to advance humanity's knowledge on the subject, and he is often redoing the work others have already accomplished.[43] Aside from being born of sickness,[44] searching for medicinal qualities involves foresight and calculation, which is the more specific form of reason that Rousseau denies to the "savage" in the *Second Discourse*: "In the morning he sells his bed of cotton and in the evening he comes weeping to buy it back, for want of having foreseen that he would need it for the coming night."[45] Foresight, as well as the passions that cause it, are "born only in society."[46] It is not always reason, simply or generally, that Rousseau finds missing in original man, but foresight that separates the civilized from the uncivilized and also goes on to make the civilized unhappy.[47]

Rousseau's innocence of foresight and calculation is further developed in his experience of time. On Lake Bienne, he is afloat "sometimes for several hours,"[48] but there is both inconsistency and vagueness to his time on the water. Rousseau does not spend a regular span of time adrift, but he instead follows his inclination. In other words, he is not drawn back by his next obligation. Furthermore, the vagueness suggests that his experience operates within a distinct *experience* of time. His reverie does not arrive like an on-schedule train. It has a different, spontaneous and indefinite, order of its own. In both cases, on the boat and along the shore, Rousseau describes himself as "plunged [*plongé*]" into reverie. We can neither control nor predict its arrival or duration. Night would often surprise Rousseau with its arrival. And if anything bounded his reverie, it was not the discrete time of a watch but the movement of nature. The setting of the sun told him that he needed to row back to shore, not the time on his watch combined with the feeling of an outside obligation. As Saint-Armand does well to notice, the son of a watchmaker, the sometime citizen of Geneva, refuses the watch, that "Genevan instrument of measurement par excellence."[49] This scene finds a companion in Rousseau's description of precivilization life, also equipped with an allusion to water, this time describing collection of humans at watering holes: "Imperceptibly water came to be more needed, the cattle were thirsty more often; one arrived in haste, and left with reluctance. In this happy age when nothing recorded the hours, nothing required them to be counted; the only measure of time was enjoyment and boredom."[50] Like his solitude, Rousseau's experience of time connects him to nature and is a rejection of man-made artifice but, more importantly, its associated obligations and foresight.

Rousseau's work as an amateur botanist, therefore, is not guided or marked by a concern for its results. In addition, Rousseau is not seeking to develop a new universal system for posterity. Rousseau does not deny that there is an order to nature, only that he is incapable of completely sorting it out, and that there is great pleasure in feeling the weight of the world around him without fully understanding and systematizing it. Rousseau gives a more detailed account of this in his third letter to Malesherbes: "Soon I raised my ideas from the surface of the earth to all the beings of nature, to the universal system of things, to the incomprehensible being who embraces everything. Then with my mind lost in that immensity, I did not think, I did not reason, I did not philosophize; with a sort of sensual pleasure I felt myself weighed down with the weight of that universe, with rapture I abandoned myself to the confusion of these great ideas."[51] The universal system of things exists, then, but Rousseau is hesitant about analyzing it. He often writes of his lowered intellectual powers in the *Reveries*, but here we see that there is a bigger principle under his lack of a unifying system. In line with our nature being a-rational, Rousseau finds the greatest delight in a feeling rather than in the experience of great thought. He still uses reason to get him to that sentiment. However, after he uses it to achieve his desired state, he can, and must, discard reason. This sentiment of existence allows him to see the greatness of being, but this experience remains a feeling and not an act of reason. In the same way that Rousseau's account of a legitimate political community involves radical denaturing in order to achieve a natural good, it is Rousseau's reason, which is foreign to original man, that allows him to achieve the peak of a natural pleasure. As Cantor notes, one benefit of botany is that it can be undergone without engaging the passions.[52] Rousseau's use of

78 | Leisure

reason, then, is further evidence that it, while not present in our original condition, may still be natural. As Derrida puts it, some of the human being's "innateness" is a "sleeping potentiality."[53] The use of these faculties opens the door to many threats to our happiness, but their development, in a controlled form, is in line with nature, and Rousseau's development beyond natural man allows him to experience the sentiment of existence beyond the capability of the "savage."[54]

Rousseau's interest in botany should further surprise us because it does not initially appear to be idle, as the activity requires motion. It is important that botany does not require a great deal of equipment or an exhausting expense of energy, but Rousseau is not quietly floating in a boat when pursuing his interest in botany but is moving about the island, is actively searching for particular plants (even if they are common rather than rare), and is codifying them.[55] There is work involved in this, and yet Rousseau tells us that botany is particularly suitable to an "idle and lazy solitary person."[56] Botany remains idle because it is free of utility and is so in three interrelated senses: it is not profitable for others, it is not profitable for himself, and it does not serve his vanity. The first two have already been discussed. Botany, at least as he practices it, is not intended to cure disease, and, unlike the study of minerals, in botany Rousseau is not seeking to become rich through the discovery of something precious. However, Rousseau's botany is also idle because he is not seeking to write a book and gain fame, to gain respect from others, or even to teach others. As Grant argues, Rousseau finds multiple sources of corruption,[57] but vanity is the most important source and is also itself the root of later corruptions.[58] To do any of those things would be to undermine the "sweet charm" of his activity.[59] Rousseau here prefigures later empirical psychology that distinguishes between internal versus external motivation. The inclusion of outside rewards tends to weaken our enjoyment in the long term, with Rousseau going so far as to say that the activity loses all that made it worthwhile, at least for those lazy and solitary creatures like him.[60]

In sorting through Rousseau's solitude and his relation to the faculty of reason, we have answered some of our guiding questions. We have found that our desire for idleness is rooted in our nature and is as much a part of our nature as our freedom. The defining features of idleness are solitude, in the form of independence from and lack of obligation to others, and the calming of reason, particularly in relation to foresight and utility. As to the method of attaining idleness, it should now be clear that it is no small task. Rousseau's idleness requires the renunciation of most of our

The Expansion of Being

sociality and its concomitant faculties. Idleness cannot be part-time; we cannot slide in and out of it for a weekend or for a vacation. Weekends and vacations still require foresight, which is revealed in our defense of such forms of relaxation. We say that such relaxation is necessary because it is restorative. But this restoration assumes a purposiveness that is antithetical to Rousseau's idleness. Such "idleness" is utilitarian, and Rousseau cannot abide.

The Expansion of Being

Though we have found a preliminary answer to why we are attracted to idleness, the difficulty of achieving idleness requires us to say more. If we must renounce much of ourselves to become idle, we must say what is to be gained by that idleness. That Rousseau is happiest while idle has already been discussed, but we must now explain the nature of that happiness, which will be found in the expansion of being and the consciousness of that expansion.

When floating in Lake Bienne, Rousseau is focused on his interior state and its motions. He loses track of time because he is absorbed with his own being. It is not enough to say he is alone—his attention is also focused inward. Botany, on the other hand, is a study of the world outside of ourselves. When it comes to this, Rousseau portrays botany as a way of blending and expanding his being: "I never meditate, I never dream more deliciously than when I forget myself. I feel ecstasies and inexpressible raptures in blending, so to speak, into the system of beings and in making myself one with the whole of nature."[61] Saint-Amand describes this as a "dissolution" of the self that "coincides with death."[62] However, this is not precise, and we should instead draw the opposite conclusion. The "forgetting" of the self is a blending of our self with other beings; that is, botany helps him experience his being connected to other beings that otherwise seem separate. The self is therefore stretched and, in this way, expanded: "I am nevertheless unable to become entirely wrapped up in my own self, because in spite of my efforts, my expansive soul seeks to extend its feelings and existence over other beings."[63] Rousseau's study of plants, then, is not a matter of forgetting the self in favor of other beings but an expansion and aggregation of those beings into his own. The study of common plants on St. Peter's Island is not simply to forget his troubles but also to see and experience his being as part of a boundless whole.[64] As

80 | Leisure

Cooper argues, the extension of being exists for Rousseau as an ultimate end, perhaps even above happiness.[65]

This expansion of being, rather than its dissolution, is also clear in the "delicious moment" Rousseau experienced upon regaining consciousness after being run over by a Great Dane: "I was born into life at that instant, and it seemed to me that I filled all the objects I perceived with my frail existence. Entirely absorbed in the present moment, I remembered nothing; I had no distinct notion of my person nor the least idea of what had just happened to me; I knew neither who I was nor where I was; I felt neither injury, fear, nor worry."[66] The out-of-body experience makes Saint-Amand's "dissolution of the self" interpretation understandable, but again the opposite conclusion follows. Despite having no notion of his person, he did not experience death but instead experienced himself as "born."[67] Further, his consciousness did not leave his person to be thereafter dissolved, but it instead "filled all the objects [he] perceived." If he loses his particularity, it is only to become everything. Making yet another allusion to water, Rousseau's narration continues: "I watched my blood flow as I would have watched a brook flow, without even suspecting that this blood belonged to me in any way. I felt a rapturous calm in my whole being; and each time I remember it, I find nothing comparable to it in all the activity of known pleasures."[68] Reconsidering Rousseau's floating in Lake Bienne, water is an important source of his expansion. While floating, the water assists his feeling that he is merging with all around him. Even listening to the water on the shore "took the place of the internal movements which reverie extinguished."[69] While the air preserves his experience of being separate from all things, water becomes the medium of his expansion, where everything merges, such as in the river of his own blood.

This expansion of being also requires purity. This is implied in Rousseau's discussion of expansion's inverse: being nothing. Consider one of the more striking passages from *Emile*: "He who in the civil order wants to preserve the primacy of the sentiments of nature does not know what he wants. Always in contradiction with himself, always floating between his inclinations and his duties, he will never be either man or citizen. He will be good neither for himself nor for others. He will be one of these men of our days; a Frenchman, and Englishman, a Bourgeois. He will be nothing."[70] Here, the problem is not failing to feel the sentiments of nature; it is the attempt to exist in *both* the civil and natural orders. The lack of purity, caused by internal incoherence, means he cannot "be" anything. The Spartan lives a very different life than the solitary Rousseau but still "is." Each life requires a dedication and purity. Therefore, Rousseau's lack of duty and foresight are necessary to his idleness. Rousseau with duty and foresight would be incapable of reverie alongside Lake Bienne. The melting of his being into others in the forgetfulness of time would be made impossible by the checking of his Swiss watch to mark the return to his Genevan duties. Torn between incompatible lives, he would thereby be unable to feel his being expanded, or even to be anything at all. Despite the seeming death of the self, then, Rousseau not only feels his being partake of everything, he also still feels, and feels a great pleasure, even if that pleasure is calm, unlike the active, ardent, and continual pleasures found in society. There is no experience of a particular self but of the self in all things. If Rousseau experiences anything like death, then, it is only to become God.[71]

The overriding theme of Rousseau's reveries in and alongside Lake Bienne is a turn, but not a *re*turn, to nature. His experience of time is not of the man-made clock but of the setting of the sun. Further, his reveries lack reason. Ideas sometime threaten his reveries, but the reveries themselves are confused and without order and coherence. Built into this lack of reason is freedom. While on the island, Rousseau follows his will and is only loosely attached to the other inhabitants on the island. He does not renege on responsibilities, and thereby do harm, because he does not enter into those obligations in the first place. This lack of responsibility allows him to follow his inclination. Furthermore, this following of inclination leads to idleness, as we see in the example of his floating in a boat and feeling the sentiment of existence for several hours at a time. As he states in his *Letters to Malesherbes*, his soul had a natural tendency toward laziness, and this laziness was indelibly tied to, and was even a cause of, his passion for freedom.[72] However, we should not let this point end as a statement about Rousseau's personal and unique nature, for this is a facet of human nature generally, according to Rousseau. Starobinski makes this point well: "By setting himself in opposition to others, Rousseau is not seeking merely to impose his own unique personality; he is making a heroic effort to live in accordance with universal values: freedom, virtue, truth, and nature."[73] Rousseau states the naturalness of idleness directly in a note in his *Essay on the Origin of Languages*:

> The extent to which man is naturally lazy, is simply inconceivable. It would seem that he lives solely in order to sleep, to vegetate, to remain motionless; he can scarcely decide to go through the motions required to keep from dying of hunger.

82 | Leisure

> Nothing sustains the savages' love of their state as much as this delicious indolence. The passions that cause man to be restless, provident, active, are born only in society. To do nothing is man's primary and strongest passion after that of self-preservation. Upon looking at it more closely, it would be found that, even among us, people work only in order to get to rest, that it is still laziness that makes us industrious.[74]

The early society of the family, it should be noted, while part of the movement away from nature, still produces great leisure. That first division of labor allows for greater accumulation of resources. This eventually takes away from our leisure in complex economies, as noted in the *Second Discourse*, but its initial result remains great leisure.[75]

As Meier does well to notice within this theme of going beyond, and not simply returning, to nature, Rousseau's idleness is also a positive achievement, not just a negative one.[76] Though Meier points to the achievement of nature and meditation as the positive achievement, the expansion of being also shows us that the development and exercise of the imagination plays a crucial role. If we were to only read the *Second Discourse*, we would come away with a wholly negative view of this faculty. The "savage" does not have this capacity, but once the human being develops it, the physical desire for sex transforms into a desire for love, creating much of our later ills.[77] However, in the *Reveries*, we see Rousseau make good use of the imagination. Combining these seemingly contradictory treatments in a coherent fashion is possible once we examine a more complete discussion of imagination in *Emile*: "In what, then, consists human wisdom or the road of true happiness? It is not precisely in diminishing our desires, for if they were beneath our power, a part of our faculties would remain idle, and we would not enjoy our being. Neither is it in extending our faculties, for if, proportionate to them, our desires were more extended, we would as a result only become unhappier."[78] The goal is, therefore, not to stifle our faculties but to guide them.[79] It is without coincidence that Rousseau immediately goes on to mention imagination, the "most active of all" faculties, which expands what is possible for us, "whether for good or bad."[80] Todorov argues that the solitary individual "inhabits the body."[81] This, I think, stems from an undue conflation of the idler with the original human. The "savage" may inhabit the body, but Rousseau, through the extreme exercise of the imagination, transcends the body. Meier's analysis rings truer, writing that the imagination liberates

Rousseau "from the bonds of the body and thus from bondage to space and time."[82] Furthermore, this controlled use of the imagination is not limited to the philosopher. Melzer makes this point starkly: "The whole point of *Emile*, for example, is to show that a man could develop his foresight, imagination, and reason without destroying his natural goodness."[83] This point, combined with the great dangers suggested in the *Second Discourse* and elsewhere, suggests that the imagination is responsible not just for great unhappiness but for expanding our happiness as well.

How Is Idleness Morally Defensible?

So far, we have seen the various ways in which Rousseau's idleness removes him from citizenship.[84] Rousseau finds duties to interrupt his need to follow his own inclinations. Furthermore, Rousseau's interest in idleness has its partial basis in circumstances that make citizenship impossible for him. And here, unsurprisingly, we must sort through yet another seeming paradox: this time between disparate claims regarding uselessness and harm. The question here is not just the possibility of achieving idleness but also its moral status. In other words, we have seen that idleness requires great capacity in the form of pushing away convention in favor of nature, but we now must consider whether doing so is morally defensible. The standard here, as always throughout the examination of idleness, is nature. The most important "moral"[85] principle of nature is the duty to not harm. This principle follows from the natural sentiment of pity, which suggests an amended form of the Golden Rule: "*Do what is good for you with the least possible harm to others.*"[86] Being a natural duty, Rousseau must therefore answer to this principle, and if idleness is to be defensible, it must satisfy this condition.[87]

At the end of the Sixth Walk, Rousseau writes: "Their wrong, then, was not to turn me out of society as a useless member, but to proscribe me from it as a pernicious member. For I admit that I have done very little good; but as for evil, my will has never in my life entertained it, and I doubt that there is any man in the world who has really done less of it than I."[88] Alone, this argument is clear and reasonable enough. Rousseau admits that he has been useless but denies that he has done any active harm. In this way, there seems to be little evidence of his idleness contradicting the supreme duty to not harm—his existence was neutral, and his relationship with civil society is therefore not troublesome.

84 | Leisure

However, this position is made difficult by a statement in the *First Discourse*: "It is a great evil to fail to do good, and every useless citizen may be considered a pernicious man."[89] The language is consistent, suggesting that this connection was intentional.[90] However, looking closely at the context of the claim in the *First Discourse*, which is the effect of science on society, science is shown to be malevolent because it goes *beyond* idleness:

> Did I say idle? Would God they really were! Morals would be healthier and society more peaceful. But these vain and futile declaimers go everywhere armed with their deadly paradoxes, undermining the foundations of faith, and annihilating virtue. They smile disdainfully at the old-fashioned words of fatherland and religion, and devote their talents and philosophy to destroying and debasing all that is sacred among men. Not that at bottom they hate either virtue or our dogmas; they are enemies of public opinion, and to bring them to the foot of altars it would suffice to send them among atheists.[91]

The "idle" actively work to destroy common morality. Science and philosophy have an inherent tendency to treat common morality and religion with disdain.[92] There is a general and particular critique being made by Rousseau here. The general critique is of the Enlightenment position that science and the arts have a positive, or at least neutral, relationship with true morality. The more particular critique is of the *philosophes*, who supported the rise of intellectuals as a social class.[93] As Mendham explains, Rousseau "never endorses [leisure] in its prevailing forms,"[94] whether it's the leisure of the aristocracy, or the idleness of the artists and scientists.

As expressed in the *Reveries*, however, Rousseau seems to portray himself as *truly* idle. Whereas the scientists and philosophers discussed in the *First Discourse* publicly disapproved of common morality, Rousseau is removed from civil society on St. Peter's Island. Thus, even if Rousseau found virtue to be an unworthy goal for his own life, his lack of vanity kept him from undermining it in others. He does not publish his thoughts on the system of nature, and, so he says, he never intended to publish the *Reveries*. This supposed lack of interest in publishing the *Reveries* often baffles readers, but the line of interpretation presented here suggests that it has to do with his lack of vanity. They are intended for his own

Rousseau's Harmless and Happy Idleness | 85

reading and reflection, to "double" his existence through reading them,[95] and not for any vain wish.[96] This does not do away with the possibility of him being insincere, but it does suggest his intent and also presents an addendum to his position in the *First Discourse*: to fail to do good is to do great harm, but only for those that are vain. Most philosophers and scientists are too vain to let common morality and virtue be. Meanwhile, Rousseau is truly idle,[97] which allows him to fail to do good without also doing great harm, at least while he is not publishing on St. Peter's Island.

The best evidence of true versus false idleness is solitude. As Saint-Amand notices, idleness is only presented as good by Rousseau when solitude is also present.[98] Solitude, at least in the form of being removed from "cultured" civil society, is necessary because its opposite, social idleness, must always be other-directed. As Rousseau explains in his *Confessions*, social idleness is a "forced labor." Social idleness, therefore, is always false idleness. Solitude is not only evidence of true idleness, it also acts as a remedy. As Rousseau states more clearly in his *Letter to D'Alembert*, solitude calms the soul and appeases the passions that social life creates.[99]

Of course, we can question Rousseau's sincerity as to his lack of vanity. There are a few passing references to a "flash of pride" in the *Reveries*, such as when he imagines himself, incorrectly, in a location no other human has trod.[100] Furthermore, Rousseau claims that the *Reveries* are for his own enjoyment, but he likely knew they would be published eventually. However, we should keep two distinctions in mind. First, a "flash of pride" should not be conflated with a vain state of being. Not all forms of amour propre are the same, with Rousseau separating a positive pride from a negative vanity.[101] We should take seriously Rousseau's discussions of his relative lack of vanity described earlier, such as his practice of botany, which was done for its own experience, rather than the pride that would come from publishing a system of botany. And second, even if Rousseau experiences twinges of pride, which he certainly seems to, his circumstances keep that in check. As suggested throughout, Rousseau's circumstances are crucial to his idleness and are so in a variety of ways. For instance, his persecution partly explains his inability to be good for others and enforces his solitude. But more importantly here, his circumstances limit his vanity. Looking again at the "flash of pride" cited previously, this event occurs precisely because he thought "persecutors could not unearth" him in his "refuge unknown to the whole universe."[102] He quickly realizes he is not in as remote an area as he thought, reminding

86 | Leisure

him that his persecutors could reach him. Thus, even if we doubt that Rousseau has internally overcome vanity, his circumstances, through his persecutors, as he says in the First Walk, have forced him to give up any hope of present, or even future, pleasure in society.[103] He may occasionally forget, but he is forced to remember. Solitude, which is enforced by Rousseau's persecution, becomes, as Davis notes, "its own solution."[104] Even if persecution partly explains Rousseau's inability to do good, the resultant solitude keeps him from doing harm and allows the fulfillment of the happiness to be found in idleness.

The lack of luxury is a second standard of authentic idleness. Luxury is born in idleness but also nurtures idleness in turn.[105] Luxury is a great vice because it requires us to forget virtue. Luxury leads to the dissolution of morals, which in turn leads to poor taste. Artists are vain, making their art worse in times of luxury, where appeals are to the lowest common denominator. However, Rousseau claims to not be infected with vanity, meaning his work does not appeal to the tastes of the masses.[106] Rousseau's idleness, therefore, is true idleness, which does not harm in the way of the false idleness of most scientists and artists. He claims to still have deserved being thrown out of society, but not because he commits great harm that undermines the virtue of the citizen. His idleness implies that he does not actively support virtue, which gives citizens the right to banish him, but he adds a wrinkle to his earlier argument that idleness is evil and pernicious.

Cantor, in a study of Rousseau's preoccupation with botany, makes the case that Rousseau carves out the aesthetic as an autonomous realm.[107] This is true in the sense that Rousseau does seem to find some goods contradicting other goods. The idler of the *Reveries* cannot also be the citizen of the *Social Contract*. But Cantor's claim is untrue if it is taken to mean that the standards of some goods are completely separate from the standards of other goods. As the no harm principle of the *Reveries* makes clear, Rousseau still requires a defense of the idle life that is consistent with his defense of other lives. We cannot be both the idler and the citizen—the two lives are certainly very different, and the citizen could not also be an idler—but they share the same foundational standards.[108] Even further, though the idler cannot be the citizen, Rousseau's justification is in the face of the claims of that citizen. The citizen claims that the idler does harm in doing no good, and it is precisely that claim that Rousseau answers between the *First Discourse* and the *Reveries*.[109]

Conclusion

Rousseau's *Reveries* paint a complicated picture. While setting up an ideal of sorts, with its claims to peaks of happiness, its value is certainly conditional, and conditional in three ways. First, it is conditional in terms of capability: Rousseau achieves true idleness because of his freedom from vanity, obligation, and foresight. Though his intellectual powers have waned, he is also aided by his great imagination, which allows him to experience and enjoy the sentiment of existence and extend his being. Second, it is conditional in that it is in tension with other goods. Rousseau misses out on the value of the citizen. However, this does not imply that he is exempt from answering to the citizen, which leads to the third way that the value of idleness is conditional: it is morally and politically conditional. Not only does Rousseau need to be capable of true idleness, he must also defend his way of life as not immoral. He accepts that he is useless but ultimately denies that he is harmful. He does no harm because his lack of vanity keeps him from undermining common morality. Salkever correctly notes that "circumscription," closing ourselves off to certain desires and pleasures, is necessary for Rousseauian happiness.[110] Many of those "goods" found in civil society, such as honor, may be false and rely upon vanity, but it nevertheless requires a certain type of soul to push away those temptations, or not be tempted at all, in favor of the standards of nature. We must ensure that our idleness does not harm, which itself is surprisingly and exceedingly difficult to accomplish. The test of this is whether we are truly interested in, and can be satisfied with, solitude. Most are not and seek to, at best, profit from their "idleness," or, at worst, harm others by undermining others' attachment to virtue and piety. We may, therefore, be free to travel to St. Peter's Island with a clear conscience, but the cost of the trip is beyond what most of us are willing to pay.

Though Rousseau's model of idleness is extreme, it is instructive, especially to contemporary ears. If it is true, as I have been arguing, that Aristotle's model of leisure is distasteful to us because of its particular form of inegalitarianism and because of its lack of concern for freedom as we understand it, then Rousseau's model should appear more amenable to our values. First, while Rousseau's model should also be understood as an accomplishment of which not all will be capable, it is not closed off to us by the class of our birth. Second, it fits more neatly with our understanding of freedom as following our inclination. However, Rousseau's

88 | Leisure

Reveries show us what that understanding of freedom means when thought through. If it is true that we are free when we do what we want, we must critically examine what it is we claim we want and ask whether, and to what extent, that desire is sincerely our own. Rousseau, for good reason, argues that many of our wants have external motivations. All too often, our inclinations are polluted by needing others to value us. As such, if we are to be free, we need to purify our inclinations from those external considerations, the core of which arise from vanity and duty.

Rousseau is right to raise this concern about leisure and our supposed interest in it. He shows us that our failure to achieve more free time is not simply a matter of economics. This was also a lesson of Aristotle and Locke, but Rousseau provides a similar insight from a concern for freedom more like our own. If my sense of self requires others to see me as virtuous, I will never have free time in a system of liberal economics. For reasons discussed in the chapters on Locke and vocation, liberal virtue is indelibly attached to work and the economic rewards of that work. As with honor in all of its forms, there is no end to it. There is no amount of work or material success that "completes" the project of vanity, but it is instead limitless. I may complain that I wish I had more free time, but I am wrong to think that more economic means will achieve it. It is only an elimination of the concern for such social value that will completely grant me that form of freedom. And it is not just the desire to be admired by others that keeps us from free time, but to the extent that such moral value in work is internalized, the concern for duty also keeps us from it. Economic activity becomes a form of patriotism in a liberal society, as that is one of the, if not the primary, forms of being useful to our compatriots. Thus, our supposed interest in leisure will always ring a bit hollow, or at least remain unfulfilled, so long as we inhabit a liberal world as full members.

Now, the very same radicalness of Rousseau that makes his *Reveries* powerfully insightful is also what makes his model impractical in a sense. Vanity as Rousseau understands it is deeply imbedded in us, as he himself recognizes. Though Rousseau claims he is free from vanity and obligation, it seems that his own natural goodness was itself insufficient and required the circumstances of his persecution in addition. Even then, Rousseau's claims about such release from vanity and obligation are themselves contestable. As such, some might conclude that Rousseau's model of idleness is impossible. However, while the extreme edge of perfect idleness may be impractical, it is not just the extreme edge that may interest us. Vanity

Rousseau's Harmless and Happy Idleness | 89

and obligation are not discrete characteristics; that is, we do not simply either have them or not. Instead, we can point to different levels of each, and those levels are of substance. If we can say that there are levels of vanity, with some possessing great deals of it, and others shedding most it, we might also say that there are levels of freedom and idleness. The extreme portrayed in the *Reveries* should still interest us as a standard, but we should not leave with the position that a sliver of vanity is the same as absolute and complete vanity.

With that in mind, we can ask how our contemporary "idleness" compares to that of Rousseau's. Even if we "fail" Rousseau's rubric, the reasons why are telling, and the stages in between complete failure and complete success are of interest. Though the discussion will not be limited to interpreting our free time through Rousseau's eyes, let us turn next to examining our own free time and suggest ways of elevating or purifying it, particularly with the example of the contemporary employment of hobbies.

Chapter 5

Free Time

Introduction

Much of the argument thus far has begun from our unfamiliarity with leisure. Reading Aristotle shows how removed we are from the classical ideal of leisure, with its focus on freedom from necessity and the moral and intellectual virtues required for active leisure. Our removal from leisure is further explained by the moral attachment to work, vocation, and the material comforts provided by work and vocation. All of this demonstrates that, even if we say we want more leisure, we are unlikely to understand what is fully implied in that saying.

A comparison with classical leisure, though, is not the only way to think through the concept. We can also analyze our closest comparable experience—what we call "free time." Though I have argued that work and vocation have replaced leisure as an ideal, free time remains closer to leisure in its claim to being free from necessity. Furthermore, the expansion of free time is what we intend when we say we want more leisure. I therefore begin again and will structure this examination around two questions: What is free time? And what *should* it become? In defining our free time, I will do so through relation, by setting it beside the models already presented: leisure, work, vocation, and idleness. As for what it should become, I consider how free time might be elevated or purified. This consideration is grounded in the aforementioned belief that any future leisure must be the product of a reaction to, or continuation of, contemporary experience and values.

92 | Leisure

Whereas the final mood of the discussion of vocation was pessimistic, the analysis of free time will be more optimistic, even if cautiously so. The reason for this optimism is that our free time offers a more fertile ground than does vocation. Let me count the ways. Vocation is failing for the reasons developed in chapter 3, but our free time does not suffer equally. Most importantly, free time does not admit of the inherent problem of combining means and ends. This point will be qualified, but the general point remains. Because we do not require our free time to support us materially, it can be undergone more purely as an end, as something done for its own sake.

It may reasonably be objected that our common activities seem both superficial and too often directed at useful ends. I share these concerns, but they share, partially, the same source: free time is still conditioned by work. As Aristotle knew, play is for recuperation, which is for the purpose of work. Despite the always present limitations, there is a defense of some hobbies as being worthy of devotion, even if, or precisely because, they primarily serve as diversions. They allow for inhabitants of liberal democratic regimes to escape, even if only temporarily, the useful. While vocation, which understands itself as transcending the useful, is still done for the sake of utility, hobbies offer a clearer break. This is why hobbies deserve a hearing. It is perhaps the largest slice of liberal democratic life that allows us to be free from utility, with no, or at least much less, guilt.

Contemporary Free Time: From Television to Aestheticism

It is useful to begin from everyday experience for several reasons, but the overriding reason here is that the best predictor of future behavior is past and current behavior. If we are looking for the future of leisure, we must consider leisure's current shape. And it is here that my optimism finds its most serious challenge. At least for Americans, the most common "leisure" activity is watching television, which accounts for more time than every other leisure activity combined, including social activities, exercise, reading, and hobbies.[1] Why have hope for future leisure if nearly everyone will simply watch television? Would we not be better working, with the instrumental forms of rationality required there, rather than existing in the vegetative state of most contemporary free time? I am not rejecting the possibility of some movies and series reaching the level of aesthetic quality as much literature. However, the point here is about common uses of free time. A glance at Nielsen ratings over the years, even when including streaming services, demonstrates that the *vast* majority of viewership is of series and programs nowhere associated with quality art. Reasonable people may disagree with whether *Breaking Bad* or *The Wire* reach aesthetic peaks, but I will assume we are not considering *NCIS* and *Grey's Anatomy* in such discussions. We watch such shows not to experience the sublime but to unwind.

The rest of the chapter will be devoted to the chances for, and methods of, achieving meaningful leisure. But a partial response to this challenge comes with lighter workloads. With heavy workloads, it is natural that our free time be spent resting. If workloads lessen, however, such a need recedes. This opens the possibility of substantive leisure, even if it does not guarantee it. But still, we must go beyond the argument that we have a right to do whatever we wish in our free time. This argument is fine, for those who argue for free time as a right.[2] However, this inquiry is not about whether, or to what extent, human beings have a right to free time. It is instead about the role of leisure in human happiness. As such, we have a heavier burden here and must examine more closely what it is we do in our free time, and also make claims about its worth. The argument about worth does not need to be about a strict hierarchy of activities. As I have argued throughout, we are unlikely to be persuaded by arguments suggesting that one choice of activity is simply better than another. Furthermore, neither Aristotle nor Rousseau argue for such a strict hierarchy. So, let us examine contemporary ways of using free time that are not simply restorative and vegetative, particularly in the form of "hobbies," which, though they do not currently form a presence equal to television in our free time, do already form a significant portion.

I will start with an example of one activity that *does* incorporate some of the substance of meaningful leisure: fishing.[3] We will turn to such an example so as to make our rather abstract discussion more concrete through the application of concepts. Furthermore, the activity is common, which, aside from making the discussion concrete, also has the advantage of allowing us to more clearly examine different *ways* of fishing. Though this may seem to overly complicate matters, this is a necessary kind of analysis. We saw it in Aristotle: not all forms of experience, enjoying, and playing music are equal. They may look similar, but some prove to be leisured and others not. We also saw it in Rousseau: not all forms of botany are sufficiently idle. It is not typically the activity simply that is of concern, but the details of *how* and *why* those activities are undergone.

94 | Leisure

We must do a similar analysis of our own pastimes. I will address fishing, in its various forms, along five dimensions pulled from Aristotle and Rousseau: its relation to rest, pleasure, utility, beauty, and its experience of time. Though the attachment some have to fishing primarily fits Aristotle's definition of play, with its focus on relaxation and pleasure, some forms, fly-fishing in particular, transcend it, and, I will argue, approach something like cultivated leisure.

We will begin with rest. On the one hand, there is the weekend fisherman who owns a boat with a large engine and comfortable seating. This fisherman is likely motivated by rest and pleasure. His boat and equipment serve to ensure both comfort and success with a lower requirement for skill. Of course, this is a generalization, but a useful one. This type of fisherman is akin to the listener of music that can only appreciate music as a method of unwinding. Unwinding, while understandable and perhaps necessary for all of us at some points, is opposed to the cultivated and educated enjoyment of music that includes understanding and appreciating beauty. But consider, in contrast, the fly-fisher.[4] He ties his own flies and he wades in cold rivers seeking trout—an elusive, picky, and beautiful fish. The fly-fisher who wades in the fast rivers of Wyoming, Montana, and Washington is not often at rest when fishing. If there is rest, it is of the variety that Locke describes when his pupil learns a trade. It is an easing of one part while straining another. Thus, the fly-fisher in a swift stream may be "resting" the parts of himself that he strains as an accountant, but he is far from complete rest.

We find a similar distinction on the dimension of pleasure. The primary forms of pleasure afforded to the fisherman with the large boat are the rest itself and the successful accomplishment of catching many and large fish. The rest is found in relaxing on a boat, perhaps with beer and the accompaniment of friends. Though we certainly do not have to regard such pleasure as corrupt or immoral, let us also not attribute to it anything elevated. Catching many and large fish is pleasant as a form of accomplishment. You set a challenge, and you succeeded. Again, we do not have to demean such a pleasure, but the chase involved can take on extreme and unsettling forms. The activity of fishing here becomes less the target than the catching, where all of the pleasure is entrusted. Like Aristotelian leisure, fly-fishing is not undergone so much because it is pleasant, but it happens to be pleasant anyway. It is often a natural result of the activity, assuming the ability to appreciate the activity as such. Its

Free Time | 95

pleasure is largely wrapped up in its lack of utility, its experience with time, and the appreciation of beauty.

As hinted in the forms of pleasure it affords, the sporting fisherman also requires his time on the water to be useful. An empty creel is a wasted day. With the goal being more and bigger fish, less emphasis is placed upon the activity itself. As such, because there is always a goal beyond the activity, and because the goal does not offer complete satisfaction—since there are always more and bigger fish—the activity will always be disappointing in the same way that Aristotle found the chasing of wealth to be disappointing and lacking in seriousness.

Of course, even most of this sporting type will not be *completely* wrapped up in the catching of fish, but much more so than the fly-fisher, who still retains the goal of catching fish, but fly-fishing inherently moderates itself by purposely ensuring a lack of success. When pushed, most fly-fishers will admit that their method of fishing is not the most effective. This, I think, is a sign that this activity is a serious contender for leisure. Because of its difficulty and, typically, its lack of success, it cannot be defended on grounds of utility. As novelist Thomas McGuane writes, "What happens to the chronic smeller of flowers, watcher of birds, listener to distant thunder? Certainly, he has lost efficiency as an angler. Has he become less of an angler? Perhaps. This is why fishermen are such liars. They are ashamed of their lollygagging and wastage of time. It's an understandable weakness. In some of today's brawny fish camps, flowers and birds can raise eyebrows."[5] Other forms of fishing require less effort and are more effective. It is only within very specific contexts that fly-fishing is more effective than putting a worm on a hook. Most fly-fishers will tell you that being on the water during these moments is special, but that is far from the only time you will find them wading in a strong current. They remain, and not because they have good reason to suspect those conditions will suddenly occur. They may have hope, but these conditions are relatively predictable. What is more, this is not rare knowledge—nearly everyone on the water understands their chances. They hope to defy the odds, but they still understand them.[6] What is still more, the fly-fisher may have a sense of disgust with those that take the utility of fishing seriously. On this, McGuane says of the "true" fisherman, "progress is toward the kinds of fishing that are never productive in the sense of the blood riots of the hunting-and-fishing periodicals. Their illusions of continuous action evoke for him, finally, a condition of utter, mortuary boredom. Such anglers will

96 | Leisure

always be inclined to find the gunnysack artists of the heavy kill rather cretinoid, their stringer-loads of gaping fish appalling."[7]

Also anti-utilitarian is the fly-fisher's relationship with time. McGuane's most famous essay, "The Longest Silence," is premised on the idea that fishing demands that its participants "waste" time. As he describes elsewhere, "Angling is extremely time consuming. That's sort of the whole point. That is why in our high-speed world anglers, as a kind of preemptive strike, call themselves bums, addicts, and maniacs. We're actually rather quiet people for the most part but our attitude toward time sets us at odds with our own society."[8] Anglers disappear for hours, days, or even weeks on end, and more often than not, return with little to show for it. They are well known as liars, but perhaps not to the end of boasting, but because they feel the intense need to justify their activity on the grounds of utility. And the truth just does not cut it. Here, sport fishing shares its greatest overlap with fly-fishing, as they also experience great "losses" of time, and it is here that it deserves the most credit. Instead of the constant awareness of the discrete movement of time found in the world of work that can never fully escape the needs of utility, the doing of something for its own sake found in hobbies like fly-fishing has an experience with time that is wholly distinct. Because of its extraction from utility, time is no longer a measurement for the angler. This is how Maclean describes the losing of a fish: "Poets talk about 'spots of time,' but it is really the fishermen who experience eternity compressed into a moment. No one can tell what a spot of time is until suddenly the whole world is a fish and the fish is gone. I shall remember that son of a bitch forever."[9]

We should be reminded here of Rousseau's experiences on and beside Lake Bienne, where the Genevan son of a watchmaker loses track of time. While he must still give way to the movements of nature, when the sun disappears behind the horizon, Rousseau does not answer to the duties implicit in the time of a watch. The angler that loses track of time does so because of the forgetting of duty in favor of inclination. McGuane therefore makes an important point about anglers being at odds with society. He calls them quiet, as in they are not political revolutionaries. But revolution is not the only way to be at odds with society, as Rousseau well knew. Good citizens are active, as in fulfilling their duties, even in a market society where economic activity itself becomes a patriotic duty.

What, then, is the psychology of these people who are often found on the water before dawn and after midnight, who wade in swift and cold streams, and who receive little compensation in comparison to their

Free Time | 97

effort? The activity cannot be explained by simply referring to pleasure, rest, or even utility. It may have some of each, but not nearly enough to explain their attachment. There are a few things to consider, each relating to the forms of beauty present in fly-fishing. First, many who fish recognize the beauty of the skill of their talented compatriots, or even of the fish they chase. It is not easy to artfully cast and present a fly beneath overhanging branches. The fly cast is also well noted for its rhythm and timing. For these reasons, the activity could be said to partake in beauty. There are romantic portrayals of this, even in pop culture, including the film *A River Runs Through It*. The expert is better adept to the aesthetic appreciation of a cast, but the film, and its success, demonstrates that even nonpractitioners can sense its beauty. Aristotle may complain that the activity is limited in its value for the same reason that the activity of a musician is. The primary value in music is to be found in the recognition of and appreciation for the form of beauty, not in the creation or demonstration of it. Still, the activity is useful on the way to recognizing fully its beauty for the same reason that music education is useful for the later artful appreciation of music.

Aside from the activity itself, the fly-fisher may contend that the trout, the fish sought by most, is itself a beautiful creature, and this beauty is revealed in and through the skillful catch and release of the fish. Aside from its physical beauty, the trout is elusive. Trout only inhabit cold and clean waters. They are very often the first fish to be killed off by pollution. Also, despite being predators, they do not have the boldness of a bass that will eat seemingly anything and everything that appears to be both moving and able to fit into its mouth. Trout do not exhibit this behavior and are most often found in shaded, and therefore hard to see, water columns, only exiting them in rare circumstances. A fly-fisher may occasionally complain about the difficulties this causes, but he will also admit, upon better reflection, that this is part of the draw of the activity, and also the beauty of the trout.

Aside from the visual beauty of the cast, though, there is also the moment that the entire process of casting is aimed at: the strike. Dry fly fishing aims at getting trout to come to the surface of the water to take the fly. Again, this is rarely the most efficient. The vast majority of a trout's feeding is done below surface. So, why do it? Because it is beautiful to watch an elusive creature gracefully rise to the surface and take a fly by rising above the water level without breaking its surface. You fish on the surface because you want to see the fish strike. It is enjoyable because

98 | Leisure

it is a challenge, but also because you want to see something beautiful. Further, the angler is in part the creator of that beauty. The angler tied the fly that attracted the trout, found a seam in the current that looked to be a good place for fish to feed, and artfully cast the fly to that precise spot. As novelist Norman Maclean writes, "One of life's quiet excitements is to stand somewhat apart from yourself and watch yourself softly becoming the author of something beautiful, even if it is only a floating ash."[10] There is an element of competition between the angler and the fish—the fisher must trick the fish into taking the fly. But that is not the essence of the relationship. The angler needs the fish to be beautiful and elusive and difficult to catch if the catching of it is to be of value. The angler requires this of the trout because the catching of the fish would otherwise not be beautiful and neither would being the "author" of its catch. Or, as philosopher Mark Kingwell puts the difference between dry and wet fly fishing:

> This is textbook fly fishing, the conventional pinnacle of the sport. One hook, one dry fly, catch and release. You need to lay that fly on the water as gently as the bug it means to imitate. Argument no longer rages over the validity of any other kind of fishing, with adherents of the wet and dry schools known to cut each other on the streets of London or refuse handshakes in the House of Lords; but we all know that the cult of the dry fly still holds sway in the upper reaches of angling's class system. Nymphs or wet flies are still dismissed as "lures," a pejorative just a short ugly cast away from "bait-fishing bastards" excoriated everywhere. Purists will tell you the dry-fly skill is not just the cast, but reading the river and presenting the very bug—and only that bug—the fish are eating. And making them come up and get it, rather than dropping it on their noses. Everything else might as well be hand grenades.[11]

The promise of hobbies, such as fly-fishing, is that they are sometimes able to push away the pull of utility. This is a portion of Kingwell's argument for fly-fishing as a serious leisure activity. It is a rare activity that allows us to escape the feeling that we should do something productive and instead focus on an activity that is worthy on its own.[12] Though I will later take issue with the extent to which this point is true, many hobbies have this character of successfully leading us away from the useful and into the profoundly useless.

Many hobbies have serious claims to deserving this level of attachment. For example, we could examine different forms of walking as more or less leisured. Like fishing or listening to music, we can separate different forms and purposes. We could walk for exercise, which does not admit of much leisure, as it aims at a goal beyond itself. However, we have alternative verbs that suggest different purposes, such as amble, stroll, or saunter. Each of these suggests a purposelessness to the endeavor. While ambling, strolling, or sauntering, we might simply appreciate the world around—or within—us. Leisure can take many forms, but I have focused on the ways in which the activity of fly-fishing deserves the attachment many of its devotees give to it. Much of it partakes in beauty, from the tying of flies, the casting of line, the strike of the fish, and the actual fish itself. In fishing, and in nearly all hobbies, devotion is required in order to achieve this beauty, but it is both present and achievable. There are costs to this devotion, and these will be discussed in what follows, but the reward is there for those that are willing to pay the cost.

Limitations of Hobbies

Despite the various kinds of promise in the example and experience of hobbies, there remain significant limitations, some more accidental to core values, and therefore surmountable, and some more perpetual, in that they are inherent to those values. The largest potential limitation is that there is rarely a full release from utility in our hobbies. Even if a perpetual issue, it is not always present to the same degree. As previously argued, the greater our release from work, the less of a problem this becomes. Still, even if our attachment to work and vocation is faltering, it is not broken, and the same values that shape our attitudes toward work also shape our free time. At least on the issue of leisure, this is where critical theorists and other forms of neo-Marxists make their most important contribution. Theodor Adorno is the most prominent voice here, and he is correct to add the following layer of depth: Capitalism is more far-reaching than creating economic incentives for more work. Its effect is deeper. First, we *feel* we must work more even if we do not. Second, it also conditions the little leisure that we do have. I will address each point in turn.

Beginning with the first point, that we feel we must work more, even if this feeling is, at best, exaggerated. Taken to an extreme, this vaguely Marxist position suggests that we are duped by the capitalists. After basic

100 | Leisure

needs are met, new needs are manufactured, requiring us to work more, even if wages increase and the cost of necessary goods decrease. As for the second point, that capitalism conditions our leisure, we are duped here as well. Our "free time" becomes merely the continuation of "profit-oriented social life."[13] Free time is therefore not free at all. We continue our economic life by shopping in our "leisure." Even to the extent that we do something not directly economic, it ultimately subserves our working lives by functioning to recharge our batteries for what is really important: laboring for someone else's profit. Liberalism, and its economic counterpart, capitalism, do much to condition our free time. Even if we are not duped by elites, the same moral posture that demands we work also demands that our free time be of economic worth, or at least a reaction to economic necessity.

Even in the case of fly-fishing, where I made the argument that fly-fishing does escape the realm of means in important ways, this escape is not complete. The activity remains at odds with what is often expected of it. When returning from a trip, an angler is expected to answer a specific set of questions. The question confronting the angler is never about how beautiful his cast was, but it is instead: How many fish did you catch? And, how big were they? Even if such questions are not internalized, which they likely are to a varying extent, the angler still confronts the standard of utility and must defend the sometimes egregious amount of time spent on the water on these grounds. Locke has convinced us that even our recreation should be useful, and we have yet to escape that influence. The playing of sports, to take another example, is not just about the enjoyment of competition, but we also defend it on the grounds that it keeps us in good physical condition.

Furthermore, this need to defend fishing, or whatever hobby, on the standard of utility, runs the risk of threatening what makes the activity valuable in the first place. It is not just that the fisher must confront others who use a different measuring stick than they do, but this measuring stick can be internalized. This may indeed be how the fisher initially defends the activity. Many first-time fishers think they will feed themselves on their catch and believe there will be a gain from their new hobby. For reasons described earlier, the fly-fisher is likely to find out very quickly that this presumption is far from correct and must develop a different attachment to the hobby. However, the yardstick of utility may force the fly-fisher into more successful methods of catching fish. But what this does is transform the activity from something done for, and worthy of being done for, its own sake, into something done for some other sake. Thus, the standard of utility is a threat to many hobbies. It affects the activity itself and also the way in which the practitioners of those hobbies understand the relationship between themselves and their hobby.

Escaping or transcending usefulness is the most important, and most difficult, aspect of improving our free time into something that could be called leisure. As both Aristotle and Rousseau suggest, usefulness is present with us in sneaky ways. On the one hand, we would likely call the viewing of unchallenging television useless, with a negative connotation to "useless" in this case. However, it is very likely useful in that it rests us from a day of toil. We do not need to wag our finger at watching low-brow television. First, because such finger wagging does little to convince us to do something else, but also it is a reasonable, and perhaps necessary, reaction to difficult labor. What might be more convincing, and also more truthful about the activity, is that we are still toiling when we watch television. It is like recovering from an injury. If I break my leg, I do not sit with my leg elevated as a fully free choice. I do it to assist recovery from the initial injury. The same is true of much television watching. It is not a free choice, but a heavily conditioned one. Work is still with you in those moments. Your employer does not have to explicitly demand that you rest after work for it to condition your activity in such a manner. One of the difficulties of defining and analyzing leisure is its many lookalikes. We might interpret Rousseau as resting in the *Reveries*—it likely looked as such to those observing him. But rest is not leisure. Rousseau was not simply resting while floating upon Lake Bienne—he was experiencing the sentiment of existence, an experience we are unlikely to have while simply resting and recovering.

The Art of Democracy

In Tocqueville's famous analysis of American democracy, we can separate what Manent calls the "nature" of democracy from its "art."[14] The nature of democracy is what democracy inclines to do on its own. Sometimes the nature of democracy is noble or just, but sometimes, when taken to extremes, democracy may become ignoble and unjust. For instance, Tocqueville found a tendency for democracies to become despotic. The logic of individualism and materialism unfolds by eroding the ties between citizens, and in an effort to remove themselves from the duties of citi-

102 | Leisure

zenship, democracies will slowly rescind freedom in favor of a heavily paternalistic state that Tocqueville calls "soft despotism."[15] Democracy, then, has a natural tendency to eventually become undemocratic. Though not always this extreme, Tocqueville was concerned with various tendencies of the nature of democracy.

The art of democracy is found in moderating some of its severe tendencies so as to make it more noble, just, and durable. Sometimes the art of democracy is found in shaping political institutions in a particular way, but more often it is found in mores and cultural traditions. For example, when it comes to moderating the "tyranny of the majority," Tocqueville's most famous example of the nature of democracy becoming problematic, the solutions are found in traditions such as local civic pride.[16] There is an institutional component to this, in ensuring local governments retain sufficient power and independence from state and national government, but it is much more a feeling of pride and responsibility on the part of the citizens to run their own towns.

The moderating of democracy is often an ennobling of democracy, but it is crucial to see that an effective moderation cannot contradict it. Civic pride works because it is inoffensive to democratic principles and, in fact, has its own claim to being democratic by appealing to the equality and freedom found in shaping and taking responsibility for our own communities. Though we do not have to construct it in terms of democracy, using Tocqueville's distinction between the nature and art of regimes is incredibly fruitful for considering the possibilities of elevating or purifying our leisure. Because the art of a regime requires that our solutions do not contradict our values, it has the virtue of also being realistic. Tocqueville himself applied the framework, though briefly, to leisure in America. Religion, he argued, provided a useful moderation to American materialism by offering the Sabbath as an opportunity to put down one's tools and concern for particularities, so as to, if only for a few hours, elevate our thoughts and concerns to the timeless and the universal. Religion had to adapt to fit the mores of American democracy more closely, but by doing so it offered the most significant source of leisure.

This chapter has been an attempt to see leisure as part of the "art" of democracy. But in order to consider fully what such an art might look like, we have to address another potential limitation of hobbies that is shared with vocation: there is little education for it. As it was with vocation, this is a particularly difficult hurdle to overcome, as it is perpetual and inherently endemic to our values. The contemporary justification for leisure is of "free" time, where we get to do what we will. Liberal values make us hesitant to admit of an hierarchy of activity, where the emphasis is on choice and personal preference for what one enjoys, not on what is and is not worthy of doing for its own sake. There is thus a danger of devoting oneself to unserious pursuits. Much of what was said in the section on vocation applies here, so I will focus on a specific component: the solipsistic nature of many hobbies. Consider the example found in the character of Uncle Toby in Sterne's *The Life and Opinions of Tristram Shandy, Gentleman.*[17] This novel should be of interest to us, if only because of its constant reference to, and satire of, Locke's theories addressed in chapter 2. Locke's theory of the association of ideas is turned against him, and the problem portrayed represents the danger of hobbies. The narrator's uncle, Toby, becomes devoted to a new hobby—the building of fortifications. However, both the choice of hobby and the resulting obsession are solipsistic. Toby previously suffered a groin wound in a battle. His building of fortifications, then, is not the result of free deliberation, it is only of interest to him because of his personal connection and history, even if an unhappy one, with military strategy. Though he eventually attempts to simulate a current siege, he begins by simulating the battle in which he suffered his wound. Toby, obviously, does not understand his obsession as simply solipsistic—he thinks the building of fortifications is of the utmost importance. He finds it to be a great service to the public, as they can be educated and informed about fortifications, which is, to Toby and his attendant Trim, seemingly valuable. No one dares tell him otherwise. Even his brother, the ultrarational Walter, who is always pained by Toby's constant and long speeches on fortifications, has too much love for his brother to hint that his work is unimportant. Walter does prove unable to hold his tongue during one of Toby's long speeches but quickly asks for forgiveness when he sees the effect of his cruelty:

> He rose up hastily from his chair, and seizing hold of both my uncle *Toby*'s hands as he spoke:—Brother *Toby*, said he,—I beg thy pardon; forgive, I pray thee, this rash humor which my mother gave me.—My dear, dear brother, answer'd my uncle *Toby*, rising up by my father's help, say no more about it;—you are heartily welcome, had it been ten times as much, brother. But 'tis ungenerous, replied my father, to hurt any man;—a brother worse;—but to hurt a brother of such gentle manners,— so unprovoking,—and so unresenting;—'tis base:—By heaven,

104 | Leisure

> 'tis cowardly.—You are heartily welcome, brother, quoth my uncle *Toby*—had it been fifty times as much.—Besides, what have I to do, my dear *Toby*, cried my father, either with your amusements or your pleasures, unless it was in my power (which it is not) to increase their measure?[18]

Walter, despite feeling his brother's activity and obsession to be worse than useless, is unable to confront his brother with this fact. Felt even more strongly than his belief that the building of fortifications is not worthy is the belief that his brother must be allowed to find his own way to satisfaction.

Not only is the origin of the hobby to be found in a painful page of Toby's own history that is of no interest to anyone but himself, his hobby-horse[19] becomes the touchstone of everything else in his life. As in vocation, hobbies become expressions and formations of our identities, and this can be taken to absurd extremes. Uncle Toby's failings are meant as a satire of Locke's theory of the association of ideas. However, it is also a commentary on the psychology of those with hobby-horses. Hobbies have a way of being imperial over our other concerns, and these obsessions run the risk of becoming our only point of association for everything else. To some extent, there is some benefit. If a hobby is worthy of serious devotion, we should be sympathetic to those who take it seriously and devote themselves to the activity. However, not all hobbies have this character. Even if we do not join Aristotle in finding some pursuits more fruitful than others, we can at least join Rousseau in the position that some activities are corrupted by vanity and the need to be "useful." This becomes an even greater danger, as we have internalized the belief that nearly nothing can supersede personal preference, as we see in a rhetorical question posed by Sterne's narrator: "So long as a man rides his Hobby-Horse peaceably and quietly along the king's highway, and neither compels you or me to get up behind him,—pray, Sir, what have either you or I to do with it?"[20] It is Uncle Toby's prerogative to devote himself to military fortifications. If his own hypercritical brother does not have the heart to undermine him, who else will?

Though the solipsistic tendencies of hobbies are related to Rousseau's concept of vanity, the issue here is slightly different. The problem is not that hobbies are only enjoyed because they help us look better in the eyes of others, though this might be its own concern, but more simply the concern is only with the self and its development. It does not hear or

Free Time | 105

see anyone else and refuses to answer to standards that come from the outside. It is so by design. We refuse to upset the sacredness of individual inclination during free time. Because of this form of freedom from outside influence, we therefore have an additional roadblock to elevated leisure. The individual may choose something more elevated than building fortifications, but we are not allowed to judge, at least publicly, the devotion to silly activity.

It gets worse when combined with the other tendencies discussed earlier. The obsessive quality of hobbies can often be a problem, but so too can its opposite. Uncle Toby, as an aristocrat, has the time and resources to obsess over the building of fortifications. He does not have a trade or job, and so he has the means of pouring himself into the activity. This is not an experience most of us have with our hobbies. Consider, instead, the example of a hobby that we may admit is worthy of the kind of devotion that Toby gives to his fortifications. Let us say that this hobby is poetry. Unlike Toby, our poet must work in order to make a living. Our poet works a full-time job and must relegate her writing to evenings and weekends. There is an obvious problem of time and energy. One reason why many of our chosen hobbies are not impressive is that we require them to be a respite from work. That most of us turn to unchallenging television after work is understandable. We need our free time to be relaxing, not demanding.

Serious activities are not, by definition, rejuvenators of energy. If they are to be worth doing at all, they require the time and energy that we devote to work. The previous example of fly-fishing operates as a kind of middle ground. It serves something of the function that Aristotle conceives play serving: it is rest that makes us better able to return to work. Fishing removes us, even physically, from the everyday. It requires that you escape, and, in this way, can serve as a break from work. But that is not all that it is. It also demands great effort. The escape itself takes effort, and so does the activity of fly-fishing.

Because of the demands of work, something like fly-fishing is the best we can, currently, reasonably hope for. It is demanding and beautiful, but it can be restful. One cannot much hope for the accountant to become a poet. The highest activities are too much, at least for enough of us for it to be worthy of discussion, which is partly why Tocqueville found America to be lacking in the arts and sciences. On this, Tocqueville argued: "There is no denying the fact that, among civilized nations today, few have made less progress in the higher sciences or produced a smaller

106 | Leisure

number of great artists, illustrious poets, and celebrated writers than the United States,"[21] and "it is impossible to imagine anything as insignificant, dull, or encumbered with petty interests—in a word, as antipoetic—as the life of an American."[22] The causes of such an antipoetic spirit are multiple, but one is the simple material fact of the need for occupation. Even if individuals become wealthy, they must keep working because fortunes are instable. Occupation means the higher activities are nearly impossible. Furthermore, it shapes the soul of those who work. We cannot expect the person who directs her life toward occupation to suddenly shift to leisure once she attains an appropriate level of wealth. Tocqueville does not go so far as to say art will not exist in democratic societies. Despite the force of the law of inheritance, and the concomitant need to make all things equal, nature revolts. The more talented will gain wealth and the human mind simply cannot completely succumb to the realm of the material. The mind is naturally drawn to the "infinite, the immaterial, and beautiful."[23] Still, their leisure is never secure or complete in the way that it was for the aristocracy. Tocqueville suggests that the genius will be able to transcend the material, but only incompletely. And if the genius finds herself weighted down with material concerns, what of the nongenius?

The question is not whether genius arises in democracy. It can, and Tocqueville knew it. America has Twain, Faulkner, and Toni Morrison. The question is over the leisured appreciation of those works. An aristocracy not only supports artists, it also supports the cultivation of their appreciation. The creation of beauty is not enough—there must also be someone there to recognize it. This is the peak of Aristotle's discussion of education at the end of the *Politics*. The point is not to play beautiful music, but to recognize and appreciate that beauty. It is here that the current critique is aimed. If a genius, the accountant can become a poet. But if not, she is very unlikely to cultivate a leisured appreciation of art. Such an appreciation, both Aristotle and Tocqueville would agree, requires a significant education. Not only does liberalism distract from such an education, it fosters its precise opposite. Even if the human mind naturally seeks out the infinite, the immaterial, and the beautiful, it needs to be attuned to each. Liberalism makes us much better attuned to their opposites. Indeed, it requires that attunement. The human mind seeks out the immaterial after the material has been secured, but such security is difficult to attain. We should find beauty in a liberal democratic world, but we will not find many worshipping at its altar. There is a symphony, but the hall is rarely full.

The highest activities require a devotion that most of us cannot give them. Poetry can be a calling, but as a hobby it is problematic. It requires an education, and its pleasures are often not as immediate as the pleasures of other hobbies. This is why I claim fly-fishing is the best most of us can hope for. Though it is not best understood as restful or relaxing to the extent other pastimes are, it is restful in its own way. Many of the charms of fly-fishing, and many other sports like it, show themselves, or at least tease us, from the beginning. Someone who has fished for thirty years may be better capable of appreciating the beauty of a cast, and also the beauty of skillfully catching a beautiful creature, but it does not take a savant to immediately sense the attractiveness of catching a brook trout in a remote stream. This experience is worthy on its own while simultaneously goading you into getting better and undergoing a more thorough education in the sport. This is not always true of poetry. Nineteenth-century Romantic poetry, with all of its allusions and references that require an impressive education simply to decode, does not always admit of initial pleasure. This is a problem for those that must work. We *can* choose hobbies that are fulfilling and elevating, but we *need* them to be accessible. And this limitation partly explains why many of our hobbies lack seriousness.

It may reasonably be objected that recognizing higher and lower forms of leisure cannot be part of Tocqueville's art of democracy, as it contradicts the principles of liberal democracy. Such a recognition, so the argument goes, flies in the face of our love of equality. However, a love of equality does not, of course, force us to desire equality in all of its forms. In the same way that a religious person could be tolerant of other views while still believing the truth of his own belief, we could be tolerant of the free time of others while also holding some uses of free time to be superior to others. Toleration is the principle that cannot be objected to in this case. As Tocqueville himself argues about the love of equality, there is a legitimate passion for it that also supports freedom.[24] This I take to be the toleration element of equality. However, the love of equality can run away from itself and apply itself where it does not belong. The art of democracy, as previously stated, is largely the ability to not take the principles to absurd ends. Free time could be a place of practice in the art of democracy, where we remain tolerant but also do not give in to the conclusion that all uses of free time are equal. Again, admitting better and worse uses of free time does not have to take a moralistic tone, especially when the standard is felicity.

108 | Leisure

A final objection worth responding to: Why not apply the same "art of democracy" argument to vocation? If it is possible for free time and hobbies to somehow admit of better and worse forms, why is that not true of vocation? While I admit that it is possible—and certainly many do recognize better and worse forms—the issue is the endemic relationship to utility. I have argued that our free time remains conditioned by the logic of usefulness, but it need not be. Vocation, meanwhile, requires that component. While it is possible, even if difficult, to allow for a useless hobby, a useless vocation makes no sense. As previously argued, vocation does go beyond some forms of utility, but it never escapes it. Weber's politician may be devoted to her work beyond economic compensation but is still attached to the good such work might do for others. While, of course, a noble goal, the benefits of leisure come, in part, from its freedom from usefulness. Vocation cannot be freed from that standard, but it is possible for our free time and hobbies to escape it, even if it is difficult to escape it completely. Transcending usefulness can be part of the art of free time, but it cannot be part of the art of vocation.

Conclusion

If greater leisure or idleness is a possible future, either individually or collectively, we must step beyond the instrumental and be *willing* and *able* to dwell with the useless. There is a lot included in being "willing and able" to be useless, and much of this book has been devoted to unpacking what it would mean to be willing and able to be such. As for the willing, we must actively desire leisure, which finds its most serious roadblock in the moral attachment to work. This attachment is more thorough than we often admit. Not only do we see work as central to our identity, we also feel the pull of utility in our free time. We must give that up to be "willing" to have leisure.

As for the "able," free time is not free without virtue of character, whether we join Aristotle in calling it moderation, or join Rousseau in calling it a lack of vanity. And just as important as those preconditions to leisure is what is done once there. A problem with contemporary free time is that we do not know what to do with it. We are educated for instrumentality, so it is no wonder that our free time also tends to become instrumental. Even if we do not join Aristotle in saying leisure is not leisure without the intellect, even Rousseau's idleness is elevated and expanded by the intellect. Being moderate and without vanity means nothing, for leisure and idleness, if we do not have the capacity for *being* leisured and idle.

Learning from Tocqueville, the development of the art of free time requires that any elevation or purification of free time be consistent with, or at least not contradict, overriding attachments. Therefore, we cannot positively require some activities over others, but this does not bar us from informally directing education down particular paths. And this is already present: note the existence of liberal education in market societies today. Proponents of liberal education may bemoan its diminishing place in higher education, and also the supposed lowering standards of those educations, but it is nevertheless crucial to make the simple observation that intellectual education, which makes little claim to directly preparing students for a market economy, exists. Assuming the preconditions to greater leisure are satisfied, in the sincere desire for more free time, liberal education can expect to remain and, hopefully, grow. Mandates are unnecessary for some elevation of free time. Such institutions already exist, even alongside strong attachments to industriousness. If we hope for free time to elevate above watching television, then, this must be the foundation of it, if that hope is to be reasonable. Even if liberalism—or civilization itself—requires some vanity and instrumentality, the fruits of leisure and idleness are dependent upon our relative success in transcending them.

Conclusion

While the question of leisure never fully closed, recent workplace developments, such as the "Great Resignation" and "Quiet Quitting," have opened it wider. I previously raised several questions that such developments pose, such as: What is the origin of our recent pulling away from work? What is the nature of our increased interest in leisure? And, what shape is our leisure likely to take? Now that we have taken a tour of the intellectual history of the concepts of leisure and work, we are in a better place to examine those trends.

I have argued that there are barriers on the path to leisure, and that these barriers are more challenging to maneuver than commonly understood. Some of the barriers are external, and others are internal. Most contemporary accounts of leisure emphasize the external. We can summarize the external barriers into the three interrelated categories of economic, political, and technological. We tend to think we are unable to have more leisure because of a felt need to improve our financial condition. In this case, we may think leisure awaits us at that improved condition, but we always seem short of the goal. Interwoven with the economic, we also think that we cannot have leisure until the political system recognizes leisure as a political right and the workplace is sufficiently regulated to support that leisure, whether in the form of guaranteed paid leave, restricted work hours, or a guaranteed basic income. Finally, the technological barrier concerns our ability to achieve economic goals, individual and collective, without labor. Perhaps, one day, assuming there is sufficient political shaping of technological progress, we think gains in efficiency and automation will lead us toward greater leisure.

I do not deny such barriers. In fact, this book has been an attempt to more fully capture the weight of them. My argument is that there are

112 | Leisure

also *internal* challenges, and those internal challenges also partially explain the external. For example, while I would agree political changes would be required for more people to have more leisure, my question is instead: What would it mean to have the political *will* to achieve those changes? Proposals for a universal basic income or guaranteed paid leave, assuming such policies would indeed make us more leisured, will require a significant change in the hearts and minds of citizens. The same is true of the technological challenges. Why should gains in efficiency and automation lead to supporting leisure rather than simply to more growth? We would need a change in value to transfer those efficiency gains toward leisure. I have attempted to uncover some of the value attachments that make such a change necessary.

One interpretation of the Great Resignation is that it reflects an increased interest in leisure. While there is some merit in that interpretation, I find the Great Resignation to be more about work than it is about leisure. I agree with Hymes, who claims that the key question is *why* people are leaving their jobs. Furthermore, I agree that such moments are *opportunities* for reconsidering our values, but I do not go so far as to think that the Great Resignation reflects a "radical rethinking" of our relationship to work.[1] I am unconvinced that there is strong evidence for a "dramatic change" in American values in the increase in resignations. In the very least, if there is a dramatic change, it does not appear to be in favor of leisure. If that were true, we would expect great numbers of workers to either leave the workforce or "downshift" into much less demanding positions.[2] But this does not seem to be happening. Instead, we are witnessing the great majority of those resigning simply because the circumstances put workers in a better bargaining position, and we are seeing them leave jobs for better-paying ones.[3] It is possible that many did consider "work-life balance" as part of their decision to leave for a different position, but there is not much evidence for large changes in our relationship to work. I think it likely that some have used the opportunity for such reflection and have indeed done such reconsidering, but that "movement" remains a relatively small one, even if growing.

In addition, much of the disappointment in regard to our work does not stem from a doubt about its appropriate place in our happiness so much as a disappointment that our current situation does not meet our expectations. As such, the Great Resignation does not necessarily suggest that our principled attachment to work is in danger. Instead, it is just as likely a reflection of our continued, and perhaps increased, expectations

Conclusion | 113

of work as a crucial component of happiness. In other words, if we are dissatisfied with our careers, that disappointment assumes an expectation that went unfulfilled, not necessarily a changing expectation.

The more complicated phenomenon here is "Quiet Quitting," the doing of what is necessary at work and not stretching beyond required tasks. It is the refusal to invest in work beyond a contractual agreement, and the refusal to depend on our jobs for any well-being beyond their contribution to our bank account. I say this is more complicated, as the reasons for it are almost certainly more varied. One experience that could lead to Quiet Quitting is the disappointment mentioned earlier. Rather than refusing to dedicate ourselves to work as such, we are simply refusing to dedicate ourselves to our current position. Vocations are democratic in a sense, as they do not bar access as a matter of inherited privilege. However, not all positions are equally sought after as vocations. Low-skilled physical labor, middling office positions, and customer service are rarely understood as having much vocational potential. However, such positions represent massive chunks of the economy, effectively leaving a relatively small set of positions with such vocational potential. While democratic in an important sense, then, vocations end up being quite exclusive. As argued, this leads to an inevitable disappointment on the part of those who were raised with the view that work would not be corrupting but would be a source of well-being, even apart from its economic rewards.

Many Quiet Quitters have likely felt this disappointment. The more complicated question is the extent of that disappointment. Of course, we will see individual variation: some will be disappointed with their current position, but others are experiencing a greater disappointment. That greater disappointment can take the form of a rejection of vocation as such, and this is why I think Quiet Quitting is potentially a greater sign of a rethinking of work than is the Great Resignation. If Quiet Quitters are still invested in vocation, even if their current positions did not meet expectations, we would expect many of those workers, out of self-interest, to keep up appearances. Success in their current position may lead to opportunities in more rewarding positions. So, either such Quiet Quitters have given up their potential access to those positions, or there is a larger distancing from work as such.

Even for those that have undergone a thorough rethinking of their relationship to work, though, that rethinking is still dominated by a *rejection of* work, rather than a positive *striving for* leisure. The emphasis is still on work, with the result that we have not spent much time thinking about the

114 | Leisure

nature of leisure. This book has been an attempt to make a pass through a few ways of conceptualizing leisure beyond a reactionary rejection of work. However, this has not been a self-help book. It does not aim to offer a five-step plan to making your life more leisured. One of the lessons of the project is that leisure, especially in a liberal world, is complex. As we saw in both Aristotle and Rousseau, an activity is not simply leisured or unleisured, which makes any cataloguing of leisure-approved activities a fool's errand. In the last chapter, the example of fly-fishing was given as a possibility, but even there it comes with all of the caveats of context, such as the motivation for undergoing it, the extent of skill, and so forth. Thus, if we see two people fly-fishing, one could be leisured, and the other not. Likewise, Aristotle gives the example of contemplation—*theoria*—as the leisured activity par excellence. However, contemplation is not simply thinking but the active and conscious possession of the highest truths. It assumes an ability to arrive at such truths, which itself assumes an interest in it, and also assumes a posture toward truth for its own sake. It would be unhelpful from this perspective, then, to simply tell someone to skip work and go fly-fishing.

But I have said that we must go beyond a reactionary attitude toward work, that we must actively and positively move toward leisure rather than fall into it as a result of turning away from work. And while there are no self-help style answers to give here, a serious reading of Aristotle and Rousseau does provide useful models, even if, by necessity, they are not of the concrete variety. In what is left, I would like to summarize what I see as the most useful lessons for our contemporary context. In other words, for those seriously rethinking their relationship to work, what would it mean to move toward a substantive leisure?

Considering what such leisure might look like, we must admit that not every form of leisure is consistent with contemporary values, especially with contemporary visions of equality and freedom. However, while some of Aristotle's ideal regime is distasteful to us, some lessons remain relevant, particularly the treatment of leisure as a "way of being." Even if we reject the "elitism" of Aristotle's emphasis on intellectual endeavors and wish to include more experience under the umbrella of leisure, I think it must remain anti-utilitarian. This is not an impossible posture for a liberal democrat, but it is a difficult one. Our education prepares us for a very different posture toward our activities, even those in free time, but leisure requires us to dwell in the useless.

Both models also present leisure or idleness as radically difficult to achieve. Even for Rousseau, idleness remains an achievement for the few. We may question, then, whether leisure can ever be consistent with concerns for equality. Will leisure always be "elitist"? Some will inevitably have an easier path to leisure so long as there are disparities of class and race. However, that is not a problem internal to leisure, at least in its more democratic forms. A world devoted to free labor has not eliminated those inequalities, and leisure does not necessarily need them. Rousseau does not need to be an aristocrat to float in Lake Bienne. But still, the forms of leisure presented here are elitist in the sense that they will be achieved by some more than others, even assuming precisely equal access. Rejecting the call of usefulness is not easy—some will be less successful at it than others, and some will not desire it in the first place. So, there is a variety of elitism necessarily associated with leisure, but only if all forms of unequal outcome are considered "elitist." But if that is our working definition of elitism, it is unclear what ventures would count as egalitarian. Furthermore, as discussed in the foregoing, vocation—the primary contemporary rival to leisure—is also elitist in some senses, and more so than leisure. Aside from unequal access to the common routes to vocation, such as education and training, I am unaware of an account of vocation that thinks everyone will achieve it, even with universal access.

The form of elitism that is distasteful to liberal democracy is unequal access by arbitrary means of fortune. While such is present in Aristotle's ideal regime, it is not present in all accounts of leisure. Furthermore, vocation is not free from the influence of fortune. Economic forces influence access to vocation, even if we assume a perfectly meritocratic society. If my calling is to be a physician but the market is saturated with them, I may not have access to that career, even if I have the qualifications. Of course, it would be unjustified to assert, conversely, that leisure has no similar economic constraints, but they are less direct than are those of the workforce. In the very least, we should conclude that leisure has no more essential relationship to arbitrary fortune than does vocation. And therefore, while I easily grant that leisure is elitist in some senses, it is not elitist in the forms that need to contradict a concern for the equality central to liberal democracy.

Dwelling in the useless is also part of the more democratic form of leisure addressed here, that in Rousseau's *Reveries*. Both models require separating the self from useful concerns, and not just for short bursts of

116 | Leisure

time—regardless of whether we use the language of Aristotle and call that dwelling in the useless a virtue, or use the language of Rousseau and call it a lack of vanity on the way to experiencing the sentiment of existence. The models provided by Aristotle and Rousseau remain relevant, then, despite their radicalness. In fact, their radicalness is useful in helping us recognize the difficulty of leisure.

Dwelling in the useless also requires that we avoid "personal development." Aristotle and Rousseau are again in agreement, though for differing reasons. Rousseau's position is much simpler. If we, in our "free" time, choose to develop our capacities, we are doing that activity for some other reason, which spoils its capacity for joy. Also, we are likely guilty of engaging in that activity for vain purposes. Aristotle agrees, which may be surprising. It is surprising because he is constantly requiring us to focus on our higher natures and the development of our higher capacities. It would seem, then, that we should work on those capacities in our leisure. The development of faculties may be necessary for leisure, but leisure is not the development itself. It is the flowering of that development. It is not the continual striving to get better, but the enjoyment of the fruit of that striving. Aristotle's leisure *assumes* excellence. Reading a classic novel for the purpose of expanding cultural knowledge may be a fine use of "free time," but that does not make it leisure. To be leisured, the reader must read the novel for its beauty rather than for personal development. Applying Rousseau to the same example, he would object that reading such a work for "personal development" is likely done out of vanity. "Cultural knowledge" in this case is likely to be to the end of appearing better than others. The details matter here. Are we reading because we want to impress those around us? Then we are not leisured. Are we reading because we are attempting to improve ourselves? While noble, we remain unleisured until we shed external motivations. The reader of *Anna Karenina* needed much development to get to the place of simply delighting in the novel, but it is not until that stage is reached that the reading of *Anna Karenina* is leisured. We can admire the student working his way toward such a reading, but he is unleisured if it is done out of obligation, or if its beauty remains hidden from him. For most of us—as a very hesitant rule of thumb—it is not until we read such works multiple times that we get to such a place. We are more likely to be leisured while rereading a favorite novel than we are when giving a difficult text a first attempt. We remember the plot and the characters and are therefore in a better position to relish the experience.

Leisure promises a state of arrival. Rather than the unending building found in the logic of work and vocation, leisure claims a spot for the active completion and fruition of that building. And as Rousseau's example suggests, this accomplishment may not involve much development but instead the remembering of our pre-labor nature. Leisure must be made to fit our values, but our values will also need to be revised for us to fit leisure. It requires a particular character, one that allows for leisure to come naturally. Until we no longer need to force ourselves to choose leisure over work, "leisure" will continue as a mere remainder in our lives and will not be leisure at all.

Notes

Introduction

1. I will be making use of the first-person plural throughout. When I speak from the vantage point of "we" or "us," I speak from the very general position of a liberal democrat, who is attached, in a general way, to the ideals of equal dignity, freedom grounded in the protection of rights, and, as will be added later, a sense of purpose connected to industriousness. Of course, not all will perfectly identify with each of the positions I attribute to "us," but that is what is intended by the use of the first-person plural in this book.

Chapter 1: Classical Leisure as a "Way of Being"

1. Alexis de Tocqueville, *Democracy in America*, trans. Arthur Goldhammer (New York: Library of America, 2004), 642.

2. Josef Pieper, *Leisure: The Basis of Culture*, trans. G. Marsbary (South Bend, IN: St. Augustine's Press, 1998), 4–5; Johan Huizinga, *Homo Ludens: A Study of the Play-Element in Culture* (Boston, MA: Beacon Press, 1955), 191–213.

3. See especially J. L. Stocks, "ΣΧΟΛΗ," *Classical Quarterly* 30 (1936): 177–87; John S. Marshall, "Aristotle and the Agrarians," *Review of Politics* 9 (1947): 350–61; Sebastian de Grazia, *Of Time, Work, and Leisure* (Millwood, NY: Kraus International, 1962); Friedrich Solmsen, "Leisure and Play in Aristotle's Ideal State," *Rheinisches Museum Für Philologie* 107 (1964): 193–220; Joseph Owens, "Aristotle on Leisure," *Canadian Journal of Philosophy* 11 (1981): 713–23; Robert C. Bartlett, "The 'Realism' of Classical Political Science," *American Journal of Political Science* 38 (1994): 393–95; Pierre Destrée, "Education, Leisure, and Politics," in *The Cambridge Companion to Aristotle's "Politics,"* ed. M. Deslauriers and P. Destrée (Cambridge: Cambridge University Press, 2013), 309.

4. For another striking example of the importance of leisure to many of the ancients, consider Plutarch: In his praise of Lycurgus, Plutarch argues that

120 | Notes to Chapter 1

the early Spartans, in contrast to Aristotle's account of later Sparta, had and were capable of leisure spent in "rational conversation" on questions of the good. They were only able to achieve this because of their rejection of commerce. Plutarch, *Plutarch's Lives Volume 1*, ed. A. H. Clough, trans. J. Dryden (New York: Modern Library, 2001), 74–75.

5. See also Destrée, "Education, Leisure, and Politics," 309.

6. Aristide Tessitore, "Making the City Safe for Philosophy: *Nicomachean Ethics*, Book 10," *American Political Science Review* 84 (1990): 1256–57.

7. See also Bartlett, "The 'Realism' of Classical Political Science," 392.

8. Marshall, "Aristotle and the Agrarians," 354.

9. Destrée, "Education, Leisure, and Politics," 309.

10. Quotations from the *Politics* come from the following edition: Aristotle, *Aristotle's "Politics": Second Edition*, trans. C. Lord (Chicago: University of Chicago Press, 2013).

11. Quotations from the *Metaphysics* come from the following edition: Aristotle, *Aristotle's "Metaphysics,"* trans. J. Sachs (Santa Fe, NM: Green Lion Press, 1999). See also Owens, "Aristotle on Leisure," 715.

12. See, for example, Stocks, "ΣΧΟΛΗ"; Bartlett, "The 'Realism' of Classical Political Science," 393; Destrée, "Education, Leisure, and Politics," 309.

13. Quotations from the *Nicomachean Ethics* refer to the following edition: Aristotle, *Aristotle's "Nicomachean Ethics,"* trans. J. Sachs (Newbury, MA: Focus, 2002).

14. Solmsen, "Leisure and Play in Aristotle's Ideal State," 216–17.

15. Carnes Lord, *Education and Culture in the Political Thought of Aristotle*. Ithaca, NY: Cornell University Press, 1982), 199.

16. Depew also argues that Aristotle intends philosophy in a more specific sense, but Depew's argument focuses on musical education in book 8. David J. Depew, "Politics, Music, and Contemplation in Aristotle's Ideal State," in *A Companion to Aristotle's "Politics,"* ed. D. Keyt and F. Miller Jr. (Oxford: Blackwell, 1991), 371–72.

17. Owens, "Aristotle on Leisure."

18. This is perhaps why Bartlett is able to go beyond seeing leisure as merely a precondition to the virtues. Though I think leisure is still more than a "half-solution" between the life of moral virtue and theoretical reasoning, Bartlett's recognition of the tension between moral and theoretical virtue coincides with an understanding of leisure that is much closer to the one defended here than most others. See Bartlett, "The 'Realism' of Classical Political Science," 393–95.

19. See also Hannah Arendt, *The Human Condition* (Garden City: Anchor Books, 1959), 15; Lord, *Education and Culture in the Political Thought of Aristotle*, 40–41; Judith A. Swanson, *The Public and the Private in Aristotle's Political Philosophy* (Ithaca, NY: Cornell University Press, 1992), 155; Aristotle, *Politics: Books VII and VIII*, trans. R. Kraut (Oxford: Clarendon Press, 1998), 141.

Notes to Chapter 1 | 121

20. See also Depew, "Politics, Music, and Contemplation in Aristotle's Ideal State," 364.

21. N. D. Fustel de Coulanges, *The Ancient City: A Study of the Religion, Laws, and Institutions of Greece and Rome*, trans. W. Small (Mineola, NY: Dover, 2006), 334–35.

22. Bartlett, "The 'Realism' of Classical Political Science"; Salkever, "Whose Prayer? The Best Regime of Book 7 and the Lessons of Aristotle's 'Politics,'" *Political Theory* 35 (2007): 29–46.

23. Swanson, *The Public and the Private in Aristotle's Political Philosophy*, 163–64. For an alternative account, see P. A. Vander Waerdt, "Kingship and Philosophy in Aristotle's Best Regime," *Phronesis* 30 (1985): 249–73.

24. Depew, "Politics, Music, and Contemplation in Aristotle's Ideal State," 364–65.

25. Bernard Yack, *The Problems of a Political Animal: Community, Justice, and Conflict in Aristotelian Political Thought* (Berkeley: University of California Press, 1993), 271.

26. See, for instance, Catherine Zuckert, "Aristotle on the Limits and Satisfactions of Political Life," *Interpretation* 11 (1983): 202.

27. This is only one part of the contentious interpretive subject of the status of politics in Aristotle's conception of the highest life. For a more thorough discussion of this issue, see, for instance, Robert Bartlett and Mary Nichols, "Aristotle's Science of the Best Regime," *American Political Science Review* 89 (1995): 152–60; Leo Strauss, *The City and Man* (Chicago: University of Chicago Press, 1978); Martha Nussbaum, *The Fragility of Goodness: Luck and Ethics in Greek Tragedy and Philosophy* (Cambridge: Cambridge University Press, 1986), 373–77; Richard Kraut, *Aristotle on the Human Good* (Princeton, NJ: Princeton University Press, 1989); Tessitore, "Making the City Safe for Philosophy"; Susan D. Collins, *Aristotle and the Rediscovery of Citizenship* (New York: Cambridge University Press, 2009); Salkever, "Whose Prayer? The Best Regime of Book 7 and the Lessons of Aristotle's 'Politics.'"

28. Solmsen, "Leisure and Play in Aristotle's Ideal State," 214.

29. Pieper, *Leisure*, 34–36.

30. See also Huizinga, *Homo Ludens*.

31. Pieper, *Leisure*, 50–60.

32. Pieper, 30–31.

33. Pieper, 31.

34. Lord, *Education and Culture in the Political Thought of Aristotle*, 79.

35. Lord, 103.

36. For other accounts of music as an end in itself, see Depew, "Politics, Music, and Contemplation in Aristotle's Ideal State"; Richard Kraut, *Aristotle: Political Philosophy* (Oxford: Oxford University Press, 2002), 200–02. For an alternative explanation, see Bartlett, "The 'Realism' of Classical Political Science," 395–99.

122 | Notes to Chapter 2

37. de Grazia, *Of Time, Work, and Leisure*, 19–20.

38. Charles Sylvester, "The Classical Idea of Leisure: Cultural Ideal or Class Prejudice?," *Leisure Sciences* 21, no. 1 (1999): 11.

39. See, for example, Judith N. Shklar, *American Citizenship: The Quest for Inclusion* (Cambridge, MA: Harvard University Press, 1998), 68; William A. Galston, *Liberal Purposes: Goods, Virtues, and Diversity in the Liberal State* (New York: Cambridge University Press, 1991), 223. But also Christopher Lasch, *The Culture of Narcissism: American Life in an Age of Diminishing Expectations* (New York: W. W. Norton, 1991), 68–69.

Chapter 2: Locke on the Necessity of Labor for Happiness

1. See especially Bruce Ackerman, *Social Justice in the Liberal State* (New Haven, CT: Yale University Press, 1980), 3–30; Galston, *Liberal Purposes*; John Rawls, *Political Liberalism*, expanded ed. (New York: Columbia University Press, 2005), 173–211; Patrick Neal, "Vulgar Liberalism," *Political Theory* 21, no. 4 (1993): 623–42.

2. See, for example, Nathan Tarcov, *Locke's Education for Liberty* (Chicago: University of Chicago Press, 1989); Stephen Macedo, *Liberal Virtues: Citizenship, Virtue, and Community in Liberal Constitutionalism* (Oxford: Clarendon Press, 1990); Galston, *Liberal Purposes*; Steven Kautz, *Liberalism and Community* (Ithaca, NY: Cornell University Press, 1997), 171–91; Peter Berkowitz, *Virtue and the Making of Modern Liberalism*, 2nd ed. (Princeton, NJ: Princeton University Press, 1999).

3. Rare contrary examples include Brian Barry, *The Liberal Theory of Justice* (Oxford: Oxford University Press, 1973); E. J. Hundert, "The Making of Homo Faber: John Locke between Ideology and History," *Journal of the History of Ideas* 33, no. 1 (1972): 3–22.

4. John Tomasi, *Liberalism beyond Justice: Citizens, Society, and the Boundaries of Political Theory* (Princeton, NJ: Princeton University Press, 2021), 57–61.

5. Tomasi, 3–16.

6. As Manent puts it, for Locke "man is not naturally a political animal; he is an *owning* and *laboring* animal." Pierre Manent, *An Intellectual History of Liberalism*, trans. Rebecca Balinski (Princeton, NJ: Princeton University Press, 1996), 42.

7. See, especially, Alan Ryan, *Property and Political Theory* (New York: Blackwell, 1984), 28; Jeremy Waldron, *The Right to Private Property* (Oxford: Clarendon Press, 1991), 147; Leo Strauss, *Natural Right and History*, revised ed. (Chicago: University of Chicago Press, 1999), 251. See also Arendt, *The Human Condition*, 17.

8. Here I am also setting aside Locke's sometimes inclusion of life and liberty into his definition of property.

Notes to Chapter 2 | 123

9. C. B. Macpherson, *The Political Theory of Possessive Individualism: Hobbes to Locke* (Don Mills, ON: Oxford University Press, 2011), 225–26; John Dunn, *The Political Thought of John Locke: An Historical Account of the Argument of the "Two Treatises of Government"* (Cambridge: Cambridge University Press, 1982), 255; Paul Marshall, "John Locke: Between God and Mammon," *Canadian Journal of Political Science* 12, no. 1 (1979): 94.

10. All references to the *Essay* come from the following edition: John Locke, *An Essay Concerning Human Understanding*, ed. Peter H. Nidditch (Oxford: Oxford University Press, 1979).

11. All references come from the following edition: John Locke, "Some Thoughts Concerning Education," in *Some Thoughts Concerning Education and Of the Conduct of the Understanding*, ed. Ruth W. Grant and Nathan Tarcov (Indianapolis: Hackett, 1996). It will hereafter be referred to as *Thoughts*.

12. For a defense of using Locke's epistemology to inform an interpretation of Locke's politics, see Andrzej Rapaczynski, "Locke's Conception of Property and the Principle of Sufficient Reason," *Journal of the History of Ideas* 42, no. 2 (1981): 305.

13. Ryan, *Property and Political Theory*, 28; Waldron, *The Right to Private Property*, 147.

14. Alan Ryan, "The Romantic Theory of Ownership," in *The Making of Modern Liberalism* (Princeton, NJ: Princeton University Press, 2012), 594.

15. Ryan, *Property and Political Theory*, 11.

16. Strauss, *Natural Right and History*, 1999, 251.

17. John Locke, "Second Treatise," in *Locke: Two Treatises of Government*, 3rd ed., ed. Peter Laslett (Cambridge: Cambridge University Press, 1988), §30. Hereafter referred to as *Second Treatise*.

18. See also Douglas Casson, *Liberating Judgment: Fanatics, Skeptics, and John Locke's Politics of Probability* (Princeton, NJ: Princeton University Press, 2011), 168.

19. Locke, *Essay*, II.xxviii.5–6. See also Peter King, *The Life and Letters of John Locke: With Extracts from His Journals and Commonplace Books* (London: John Childs and Son, 1858), 311.

20. Sterling Lamprecht, *The Moral and Political Philosophy of John Locke* (New York: Columbia University Press, 1918), 91.

21. Locke, *Essay*, II.xxi.48.

22. Locke, *Essay*, I.iii.3–4.

23. John Locke, "First Treatise," in *Locke: Two Treatises of Government*, 3rd ed., ed. Peter Laslett (Cambridge: Cambridge University Press, 1988), §86. Hereafter cited as *First Treatise*.

24. Locke, *First Treatise*, §58.

25. See also Peter C. Myers, *Our Only Star and Compass* (Lanham, MD: Rowman & Littlefield, 1999), 125; Uday Singh Mehta, *The Anxiety of Freedom: Imagination and Individuality in Locke's Political Thought* (Ithaca, NY: Cornell

124 | Notes to Chapter 2

University Press, 1992), 80–118; Thomas L. Pangle, *The Spirit of Modern Republicanism: The Moral Vision of the American Founders and the Philosophy of Locke* (Chicago: University of Chicago Press, 1988), 179–81.

26. The relative force of outside influence in the education of the Lockean pupil is of controversy. See, for example, John Baltes, "Locke's Inverted Quarantine: Discipline, Panopticism, and the Making of the Liberal Subject," *Review of Politics* 75, no. 2 (2013): 173–92; Hina Nazar, "Locke, Education, and 'Disciplinary Liberalism,'" *Review of Politics* 79, no. 2 (2017): 215–38; Rita Koganzon, "'Contesting the Empire of Habit': Habituation and Liberty in Lockean Education," *American Political Science Review* 110, no. 3 (August 2016): 547–58; Joseph Carrig, "Liberal Impediments to Liberal Education: The Assent to Locke," *Review of Politics* 63, no. 1 (2001): 41–76.

27. Charles Taylor, *Sources of the Self: The Making of the Modern Identity* (Cambridge: Cambridge University Press, 1989), 173.

28. Taylor, 160–61.

29. Taylor, 166.

30. Locke, *Essay*, II.i.25; II.ii.2; II.xxx.3.

31. Locke, *Essay*, II.xii.1.

32. Locke, *Second Treatise*, §40.

33. Taylor, 166.

34. Taylor, 173.

35. Galston, *Liberal Purposes*, 229; Rogers M. Smith, *Liberalism and American Constitutional Law* (Cambridge, MA: Harvard University Press, 1985), 200.

36. Locke, *Essay*, I.iv.15.

37. Locke, *Essay*, II.i.10.

38. Locke, *Thoughts*, §208.

39. Locke, *Essay*, "Epistle to the Reader."

40. Locke, *Essay*, II.xxi.32.

41. Locke, *Essay*, "Epistle to the Reader."

42. Locke, *Thoughts*, §201.

43. Dunn, *The Political Thought of John Locke*, 250–53.

44. John Locke, "Of the Conduct of the Understanding," in *Some Thoughts Concerning Education and Of the Conduct of the Understanding*, ed. Ruth Weissbourd Grant and Nathan Tarcov (Indianapolis: Hackett, 1996), §§7–8, 19. Hereafter cited as *Conduct*.

45. Marshall, "John Locke," 86–90.

46. That Locke's thoughts on education are intended for the gentry is made clear in the dedication.

47. Locke, *Thoughts*, §201.

48. Locke, *Thoughts*, §§206–07.

49. Locke, *Thoughts*, §130.

50. Locke, *Thoughts*, §207.

Notes to Chapter 2 | 125

51. Locke, *Thoughts*, §74.

52. Aristotle, *Metaphysics*, 981b14–25, in *Aristotle: Selections*, trans. Terence Irwin and Gail Fine (Indianapolis: Hackett, 1995).

53. Locke, *Thoughts*, §206.

54. Locke, *Thoughts*, §208.

55. Locke, *Thoughts*, §204.

56. Locke, *Thoughts*, §207.

57. This, of course, marks the beginning of Tocqueville's analysis. Tocqueville, *Democracy in America*, 52–59.

58. Locke, *Thoughts*, §204.

59. Locke, *Thoughts*, §207.

60. Locke, *Thoughts*, §§210–11.

61. Locke, *Second Treatise*, §28.

62. Locke, *Second Treatise*, §28.

63. See also Myers, *Our Only Star and Compass*, 166; Strauss, *Natural Right and History*, 1999, 244.

64. Neal Wood, *The Politics of Locke's Philosophy: A Social Study of "An Essay Concerning Human Understanding"* (Berkeley: University of California Press, 1983), 148; Stanley C. Brubaker, "Coming into One's Own: John Locke's Theory of Property, God, and Politics," *Review of Politics* 74, no. 2 (2012): 225–26; Michael P. Zuckert, *The Natural Rights Republic: Studies in the Foundation of the American Political Tradition* (Notre Dame, IN: University of Notre Dame Press, 1997), 275–88.

65. Locke, *Thoughts*, §206.

66. Locke, *Essay*, I.iv.15.

67. Locke, *Essay*, IV.xvi.4.

68. Peter C. Myers, *Frederick Douglass: Race and the Rebirth of American Liberalism* (Lawrence: University Press of Kansas, 2008), 25.

69. Frederick Douglass, *Narrative of the Life of Frederick Douglass* (Mineola, NY: Dover, 1995), 45.

70. Douglass, 38.

71. Douglass, 44.

72. "A slave who would work during the holidays was considered by our masters as scarcely deserving them. He was regarded as one who rejected the favor of his master. It was deemed a disgrace not to get drunk at Christmas." Douglass, 44.

73. Douglass, 43.

74. Douglass, 61.

75. Frederick Douglass, "A Friendly Word to Maryland," in *The Frederick Douglass Papers: Volume 4, Series One: Speeches, Debates, and Interviews, 1864–80*, ed. John W. Blassingame and John R. McKivigan IV (New Haven, CT: Yale University Press, 1991), 50.

126 | Notes to Chapter 3

76. Douglass, 50.

77. Frederick Douglass, "Third Annual Fair of the Tennessee Colored Agricultural and Mechanical Association" (Nashville, TN, September 18, 1873).

78. Waldo E. Martin Jr., *The Mind of Frederick Douglass* (Chapel Hill: University of North Carolina Press, 1984), 71–72.

79. Douglass, *Narrative of the Life of Frederick Douglass*, 44.

80. Douglass, "Third Annual Fair of the Tennessee Colored Agricultural and Mechanical Association."

81. Locke, *Second Treatise*, §34.

82. Joshua Foa Dienstag, "Serving God and Mammon: The Lockean Sympathy in Early American Political Thought," *American Political Science Review* 90, no. 3 (1996): 503, https://doi.org/10.2307/2082605.

83. Locke, *Essay*, II.xxi.48; IV.xx.6.

Chapter 3: Vocation and the Radicalization of Labor

1. Dennis K. Mumby, "Work: What Is It Good For? (Absolutely Nothing)—a Critical Theorist's Perspective," *Industrial and Organizational Psychology* 12, no. 4 (2019): 429–43.

2. Alain de Botton, *The Pleasures and Sorrows of Work* (New York: Vintage, 2010), 326.

3. Max Weber, *The Protestant Ethic and the Spirit of Capitalism: And Other Writings*, ed. Peter Baehr and Gordon C. Wells (New York: Penguin Classics, 2002), 120–21.

4. Max Weber, *The Vocation Lectures*, ed. David Owen and Tracy B. Strong, trans. Rodney Livingstone (Indianapolis: Hackett, 2004), 40.

5. Weber, 40.

6. Tocqueville, *Democracy in America*, 519.

7. Weber, *The Vocation Lectures*, 42.

8. Weber, 10. See also Weber, *The Protestant Ethic and the Spirit of Capitalism*, 13.

9. Weber, *The Vocation Lectures*, 10.

10. The term translated as "science" is *Wissenschaft*, which is often broader than the English usage of "science." As Owen, Strong, and Livingstone note in their edition of *The Vocation Lectures*, *Wissenschaft* can refer to any body of knowledge. It is therefore often better to render it as "scholarship" or "studies." See Weber, 1.

11. Weber, 7. I will later address Weber's commentary on this interaction: "I, at least, have found only a handful of people who have survived this process without injury to their personality."

12. Weber, 11.

13. Weber, 11.

Notes to Chapter 3 | 127

14. Weber, 12.

15. Weber, 16.

16. Weber, 17.

17. Marianne Weber, *Max Weber: Ein Lebensbild* (Tübingen: Mohr Siebeck, 1984).

18. Weber, *The Vocation Lectures*, 92.

19. Weber, 83.

20. Weber, 86.

21. Weber, 92.

22. Weber, 78.

23. Stephen Turner, introduction to *The Cambridge Companion to Weber* (Cambridge: Cambridge University Press, 2000), 16–17.

24. Turner, 17.

25. Weber, *The Vocation Lectures*, 86–91.

26. Weber, 76.

27. See, for example, Bradley E. Starr, "The Structure of Max Weber's Ethic of Responsibility," *Journal of Religious Ethics* 27, no. 3 (1999): 407–34.

28. Shalini Satkunanandan, "Max Weber and the Ethos of Politics beyond Calculation," *American Political Science Review* 108, no. 1 (2014): 169–81.

29. Weber, *The Vocation Lectures*, 92.

30. Weber, 92.

31. See also Starr, "The Structure of Max Weber's Ethic of Responsibility," 430.

32. Weber, *The Vocation Lectures*, 77.

33. Weber, 77.

34. Weber, 9.

35. Weber, 10.

36. Weber, 10.

37. Weber, 10; Harvey Goldman, *Max Weber and Thomas Mann: Calling and the Shaping of the Self* (Berkeley: University of California Press, 1988), 146.

38. Goldman, *Max Weber and Thomas Mann: Calling and the Shaping of the Self*, 144.

39. Goldman, 145.

40. Goldman, 142–45.

41. Goldman, 142.

42. See, for example, Koganzon, "Contesting the Empire of Habit."

43. Goldman, *Max Weber and Thomas Mann*, 131. On this process of secularization, see Jane Dawson, "A History of Vocation: Tracing a Keyword of Work, Meaning, and Moral Purpose," *Adult Education Quarterly* 55, no. 3 (2005): 220–31.

44. Weber, *The Vocation Lectures*, 27.

45. Weber, *The Protestant Ethic and the Spirit of Capitalism*, 11.

46. Zygmunt Baumann, *Work, Consumerism and the New Poor* (Buckingham: Open University Press, 1998), 34.

128 | Notes to Chapter 4

47. Goldman, *Max Weber and Thomas Mann*, 166.

48. Goldman, 165–68.

49. Weber, *The Protestant Ethic and the Spirit of Capitalism*, 120.

50. Strauss, *Natural Right and History*, 1999, 48.

51. Frank Martela and Anne B. Pessi, "Significant Work Is about Self-Realization and Broader Purpose: Defining the Key Dimensions of Meaningful Work," *Frontiers in Psychology* 9 (2018), https://doi.org/10.3389/fpsyg.2018.00363.

52. Mark R. Lepper, David Greene, and Richard E. Nisbett, "Undermining Children's Intrinsic Interest with Extrinsic Reward: A Test of the 'Overjustification' Hypothesis," *Journal of Personality and Social Psychology* 28, no. 1 (1973): 129–37.

53. Wendell Berry, *Hannah Coulter* (Berkeley, CA: Counterpoint Press, 2005), 132.

54. A partisan of vocation could here say that those that fail at vocation fail less than those who fail at leisure. The aristocrat who proves incapable of leisure becomes a drunk and a gambler, while those who fail to have a vocation likely remain useful. I think this is likely true, and it is in line with the modern tendency to lower the ceiling—but also raise the floor of both aspiration and attainment.

55. de Botton, *The Pleasures and Sorrows of Work*, 78. For an overview of empirical literature on the subject, see Martela and Pessi, "Significant Work Is about Self-Realization and Broader Purpose."

56. See, for instance, Beckie Supiano, "How Liberal-Arts Majors Fare over the Long Haul," *Chronicle of Higher Education*, January 22, 2014, https://www.chronicle.com/article/How-Liberal-Arts-Majors-Fare/144133.

57. Parker J. Palmer, *Let Your Life Speak: Listening for the Voice of Vocation* (San Francisco: Jossey-Bass, 2000), 3.

58. Palmer, 4.

59. Palmer, 6.

60. Palmer, 5.

61. Palmer, 54.

62. Palmer, 30–31.

63. Roland Paulsen, *Empty Labor: Idleness and Workplace Resistance* (Cambridge: Cambridge University Press, 2014).

Chapter 4: Rousseau's Harmless and Happy Idleness

1. Hereafter referred to simply as the *Reveries*.

2. Joel Schwartz, *The Sexual Politics of Jean-Jacques Rousseau* (Chicago: University of Chicago Press, 1984), 142.

3. Jean-Jacques Rousseau, *The Reveries of the Solitary Walker*, trans. Charles E. Butterworth (Indianapolis: Hackett, 1992), 64.

Notes to Chapter 4 | 129

4. Rousseau, 66.

5. Rousseau, 69.

6. Rousseau, 66.

7. Rousseau, 66.

8. Rousseau, 67. As Cooper argues, the conscious experience of our existence is the peak form of the sentiment of existence. Laurence D. Cooper, *Rousseau, Nature, and the Problem of the Good Life* (University Park: Pennsylvania State University Press, 1999), 24.

9. Leo Strauss, *Natural Right and History* (Chicago: University of Chicago Press, 1953), 292.

10. Rousseau, *The Reveries of the Solitary Walker*, 69.

11. Jean-Jacques Rousseau, *The First and Second Discourses*, ed. Roger D. Masters, trans. Roger D. Masters and Judith R. Masters (New York: St. Martin's Press, 1964), 179.

12. See also Arthur M. Melzer, *The Natural Goodness of Man: On the System of Rousseau's Thought* (Chicago: University of Chicago Press, 1990), 45.

13. Jean-Jacques Rousseau, *Emile: Or On Education*, ed. Christopher Kelly, trans. Allan Bloom (Hanover, NH: Dartmouth College Press, 2009), 39–40.

14. Rousseau, *The First and Second Discourses*, 142.

15. Jonathan Marks, *Perfection and Disharmony in the Thought of Jean-Jacques Rousseau* (Cambridge: Cambridge University Press, 2005), 86.

16. Rousseau, *The First and Second Discourses*, 142.

17. Jonathan Marks, "Who Lost Nature? Rousseau and Rousseauism," *Polity* 34, no. 4 (June 1, 2002): 479–502.

18. Rousseau, *The Reveries of the Solitary Walker*, 66.

19. See, for example, Matthew D. Mendham, "Gentle Savages and Fierce Citizens against Civilization: Unraveling Rousseau's Paradoxes," *American Journal of Political Science* 55, no. 1 (2011): 177–78.

20. Rousseau, *The Reveries of the Solitary Walker*, 66.

21. Jean-Jacques Rousseau, "Letters to Malesherbes," in *The Confessions: And Correspondence, Including the Letters to Malesherbes*, ed. Christopher Kelly, Roger D. Masters, and Peter G. Stillman, trans. Christopher Kelly, The Collected Writings of Rousseau 5 (Hanover, NH: University Press of New England, 1995), 573.

22. Ruth W. Grant, *Hypocrisy and Integrity: Machiavelli, Rousseau, and the Ethics of Politics* (Chicago: University of Chicago Press, 1997), 144.

23. Grant, 164.

24. Rousseau, *The Reveries of the Solitary Walker*, 74–75.

25. Rousseau, *Emile*, 215.

26. Paul Cantor, "The Metaphysics of Botany: Rousseau and the New Criticism of Plants," *Southwest Review* 70, no. 3 (1985): 376; Michael Davis, *The Autobiography of Philosophy* (Lanham, MD: Rowman & Littlefield, 1999), 195.

130 | Notes to Chapter 4

27. Rousseau, *The Reveries of the Solitary Walker*, 66.

28. Joseph H. Lane, "Reverie and the Return to Nature: Rousseau's Experience of Convergence," *Review of Politics* 68, no. 3 (2006): 483.

29. Rousseau, *The Reveries of the Solitary Walker*, 66.

30. Rousseau, 67.

31. Rousseau, *The First and Second Discourses*, 114.

32. Aristotle, *Aristotle's "Nicomachean Ethics,"* trans. Robert C. Bartlett and Susan D. Collins (Chicago: University of Chicago Press, 2012), 1177b.

33. Rousseau, *The Reveries of the Solitary Walker*, 67.

34. Aristotle, *Aristotle's "Nicomachean Ethics,"* 11776b–77a.

35. Jean-Jacques Rousseau, "Last Reply," in *The First and Second Discourses and Essay on the Origin of Languages* (New York: Harper & Row, 1986), 84.

36. For a discussion of Rousseau's replacing the classical definition of humanity as rational with a definition of humanity as free agent, see Leo Strauss, "On the Intention of Rousseau," *Social Research* 14, no. 1 (1947): 487; Manent, *An Intellectual History of Liberalism*, 77.

37. Roger D. Masters, *The Political Philosophy of Rousseau* (Princeton, NJ: Princeton University Press, 1968), 351.

38. John Locke, "Second Treatise," 270–71.

39. Masters, *The Political Philosophy of Rousseau*, 324.

40. Rousseau, *The Reveries of the Solitary Walker*, 90.

41. Rousseau, 92–93; Christopher Kelly, "Rousseau and the Case against (and for) the Arts," in *The Legacy of Rousseau*, ed. Clifford Orwin and Nathan Tarcov (Chicago: University of Chicago Press, 1997), 36.

42. Rousseau, *The Reveries of the Solitary Walker*, 94.

43. Rousseau, 90.

44. Davis, *The Autobiography of Philosophy*, 217.

45. Rousseau, *The First and Second Discourses*, 117.

46. Jean-Jacques Rousseau, "Essay on the Origin of Languages," in *The First and Second Discourses and Essay on the Origin of Languages*, trans. Victor Gourevitch (New York: Harper & Row, 1986), 266n1.

47. As Starobinski notes, Rousseau is not a critic of reason as a whole. Jean Starobinski, *Jean-Jacques Rousseau: Transparency and Obstruction*, trans. Arthur Goldhammer (Chicago: University of Chicago Press, 1988), 41.

48. Rousseau, *The Reveries of the Solitary Walker*, 66.

49. Pierre Saint-Amand, *The Pursuit of Laziness: An Idle Interpretation of the Enlightenment* (Princeton, NJ: Princeton University Press, 2011), 67; Jean-Jacques Rousseau, *Letter to D'Alembert and Writings for the Theater*, ed. Christopher Kelly and Allan Bloom, trans. Allan Bloom (Hanover, NH: University Press of New England, 2004), 319.

50. Rousseau, "Essay on the Origin of Languages," 201.

51. Rousseau, "Letters to Malesherbes," 579.

Notes to Chapter 4 | 131

52. Cantor, "The Metaphysics of Botany," 371; Rousseau, *The Reveries of the Solitary Walker*, 98–99.

53. Jacques Derrida, *Of Grammatology*, trans. Gayatri Chakravorty Spivak (Baltimore: Johns Hopkins University Press, 2016), 201. See also Marks, *Perfection and Disharmony in the Thought of Jean-Jacques Rousseau*, 38. For a contrary interpretation, see Schwartz, *The Sexual Politics of Jean-Jacques Rousseau*, 100–01.

54. Benjamin Storey, "Rousseau and the Problem of Self-Knowledge," *Review of Politics* 71, no. 2 (2009): 268.

55. Rousseau, *The Reveries of the Solitary Walker*, 98.

56. Rousseau, 98.

57. Grant, *Hypocrisy and Integrity*, 143.

58. Grant, 153.

59. Rousseau, *The Reveries of the Solitary Walker*, 89–99; Schwartz, *The Sexual Politics of Jean-Jacques Rousseau*, 98.

60. For the most influential and famous evidence of this phenomenon, see Lepper, Greene, and Nisbett, "Undermining Children's Intrinsic Interest with Extrinsic Reward."

61. Rousseau, *The Reveries of the Solitary Walker*, 95.

62. Saint-Amand, *The Pursuit of Laziness*, 75.

63. Rousseau, *The Reveries of the Solitary Walker*, 95. Schwartz suggests that Rousseau's interest in botany, and in the expansion of his being through the study of plants over relations with other humans, is due in part to the examples of plants that are self-sufficient without sexuality. Schwartz, *The Sexual Politics of Jean-Jacques Rousseau*, 111–12.

64. Melzer, *The Natural Goodness of Man*, 90; Cooper, *Rousseau, Nature, and the Problem of the Good Life*.

65. Laurence D. Cooper, *Eros in Plato, Rousseau, and Nietzsche: The Politics of Infinity* (University Park: Pennsylvania State University Press, 2008), 153.

66. Rousseau, *The Reveries of the Solitary Walker*, 16.

67. Davis makes a similar point when interpreting Rousseau's floating in Lake Bienne. On his account, Rousseau rows back to shore at the sight of evening so as to flee the darkness of death. Davis, *The Autobiography of Philosophy*, 177.

68. Rousseau, *The Reveries of the Solitary Walker*, 16.

69. As Grace points out, Rousseau's reveries are almost inhuman. See Eve Grace, "The Restlessness of 'Being': Rousseau's Protean Sentiment of Existence," *History of European Ideas* 27, no. 2 (January 1, 2001): 150–51. The Godlike pleasure of reverie is made explicit by Rousseau in *The Reveries of the Solitary Walker*, 67.

70. Rousseau, *Emile*, 164.

71. Rousseau, *The Reveries of the Solitary Walker*, 69.

72. Rousseau, "Letters to Malesherbes," 573.

73. Starobinski, *Jean-Jacques Rousseau*, 40.

74. Rousseau, "Essay on the Origin of Languages," 266.

132 | Notes to Chapter 4

75. Rousseau, *The First and Second Discourses*, 147.

76. Heinrich Meier, *On the Happiness of the Philosophic Life: Reflections on Rousseau's Rêveries in Two Books*, trans. Robert Berman (Chicago: University of Chicago Press, 2016), 15–16.

77. Rousseau, *The First and Second Discourses*, 135.

78. Rousseau, *Emile*, 80.

79. Rousseau, 325.

80. Rousseau, 80–81.

81. Tzvetan Todorov, *Frail Happiness*, trans. John T. Scott and Robert D. Zaretsky (University Park: Penn State University Press, 2001), 18.

82. Meier, *On the Happiness of the Philosophic Life*, 133.

83. Melzer, *The Natural Goodness of Man*, 54n8.

84. David Gauthier, *Rousseau: The Sentiment of Existence* (Cambridge: Cambridge University Press, 2006), 175.

85. I place "moral" in scare quotes here because the context of this principle of nature is pre-morality in the state of nature. However, this principle does develop as a base of morality in the eventual development of society, where, as shown in the *First Discourse*, and discussed later, the supposed problem of idleness is that failing to do good is a great evil.

86. Rousseau, *The First and Second Discourses*, 133.

87. Judith N. Shklar, *Men and Citizens: A Study of Rousseau's Social Theory* (London: Cambridge University Press, 1985), 46.

88. Rousseau, *The Reveries of the Solitary Walker*, 84.

89. Rousseau, *The First and Second Discourses*, 49.

90. Victor Gourevitch, "A Provisional Reading of Rousseau's 'Reveries of the Solitary Walker,'" *Review of Politics* 74, no. 3 (2012): 507.

91. Rousseau, *The First and Second Discourses*, 50.

92. Jeff J. S. Black, *Rousseau's Critique of Science: A Commentary on the Discourse on the Sciences and the Arts* (Lanham, MD: Lexington Books, 2009), 175–76.

93. Michael Locke McLendon, "Rousseau, Amour Propre, and Intellectual Celebrity," *Journal of Politics* 71, no. 2 (2009): 510; Dena Goodman, *The Republic of Letters: A Cultural History of the French Enlightenment* (Ithaca, NY: Cornell University Press, 1994), 35–39; Mark Hulliung, *The Autocritique of Enlightenment: Rousseau and the Philosophes* (Cambridge, MA: Harvard University Press, 1994), 88–94.

94. Matthew D. Mendham, "Rebuking the Enlightenment Establishments, Bourgeois and Aristocratic: Rousseau's Ambivalence about Leisure," in *The Palgrave Handbook of Leisure Theory*, ed. Karl Spracklen et al. (London: Palgrave Macmillan, 2017), 273.

95. Rousseau, *The Reveries of the Solitary Walker*, 7.

Notes to Chapter 4 | 133

96. Charles E. Butterworth, "Interpretive Essay," in *The Reveries of the Solitary Walker* (Indianapolis: Hackett, 1992), 160.

97. Strauss, "On the Intention of Rousseau," 478.

98. Saint-Amand, *The Pursuit of Laziness*, 60.

99. Rousseau, *Letter to D'Alembert and Writings for the Theater*, 256.

100. Rousseau, *The Reveries of the Solitary Walker*, 100.

101. Jean-Jacques Rousseau, *The Plan for Perpetual Peace, On the Government of Poland, and Other Writings on History and Politics* (Hanover, NH: Dartmouth College Press, 2011), 154.

102. Rousseau, *The Reveries of the Solitary Walker*, 100.

103. Rousseau, 4.

104. Davis, *The Autobiography of Philosophy*, 127.

105. Rousseau, *The First and Second Discourses*, 50.

106. As Kelly persuasively argues, the *Confessions* and the *Reveries* offer the possibility of overcoming vanity. Christopher Kelly, *Rousseau's Exemplary Life: The "Confessions" as Political Philosophy* (Ithaca, NY: Cornell University Press, 1987), 73.

107. Cantor, "The Metaphysics of Botany," 363.

108. Cooper, *Rousseau, Nature, and the Problem of the Good Life*.

109. There are other notable attempts to address the civic responsibilities of a solitary individual. In the American context, the Transcendentalists offer a provocative account. For a good overview of this tradition, see Steven F. Pittz, "Identity and the Practice of American Citizenship: From Transcendentalists to Identitarians," in *American Citizenship and Constitutionalism in Principle and Practice*, ed. Steven F. Pittz and Joseph Postell (Norman: University of Oklahoma Press, 2022), 56–82.

110. Stephen G. Salkever, "Rousseau & the Concept of Happiness," *Polity* 11, no. 1 (1978): 40.

Chapter 5: Free Time

1. Rachel Krantz-Kent, "Television, Capturing America's Attention at Prime Time and Beyond," *Beyond the Numbers* 7, no. 14 (September 2018), https://www.bls.gov/opub/btn/volume-7/television-capturing-americas-attention.htm.

2. A persuasive argument for such is found in Julie Rose, *Free Time* (Princeton, NJ: Princeton University Press, 2016).

3. For another defense of fishing as a worthy activity of leisure, see Mark Kingwell, *Catch and Release: Trout Fishing and the Meaning of Life* (New York: Penguin Books, 2004). Kingwell argues that fishing uniquely, though obviously not exclusively, allows for theoretical reflection. For a related treatment of hunting,

134 | Notes to Chapter 4

see Jose Ortega y Gasset, *Meditations on Hunting*, trans. Howard B. Wescott (New York: Charles Scribner's Sons, 1986).

4. I will again emphasize that it is not the activity simply that meets the standard of leisure, but there are other factors involved. I am using generalizations here, not attempting to say that all fly-fishers are leisured and that it is impossible for bass fishers to be leisured. Fly-fishing is also used in part because of the significant literature on it as leisure activity, which will be discussed in what follows.

5. See also Thomas McGuane, *The Longest Silence: A Life in Fishing* (New York: Vintage, 1999), xii.

6. McGuane would take issue with this point about fully understanding the odds: "I'm afraid that the best angling is always a respite from burden. Good anglers should lead useful lives, and useful lives are marked by struggle, and difficulty, and even pain. Perhaps the agony of simple mortality should be enough. But probably it is not. As they say in South America, everyone knows that they are going to die; yet nobody believes it. Human lapses of this kind enable us to fish, fornicate, overeat, and bet on the horses." McGuane, x.

7. McGuane, 121.

8. McGuane, xiii.

9. Norman Maclean, *A River Runs Through It and Other Stories* (Chicago: University of Chicago Press, 2001), 44.

10. Maclean, 43. For a philosophic rather than poetic account of the fly cast, see Kingwell, *Catch and Release*, 131.

11. Mark Kingwell, *Measure Yourself against the Earth* (Windsor, ON: Biblioasis, 2015), 253.

12. Kingwell, *Catch and Release*, 196.

13. Theodor W. Adorno, *The Culture Industry: Selected Essays on Mass Culture*, ed. J. M. Bernstein (New York: Routledge, 1991), 180.

14. Pierre Manent, *Tocqueville and the Nature of Democracy*, trans. John Waggoner (Lanham, MD: Rowman & Littlefield, 1996), 26.

15. Tocqueville, *Democracy in America*, 816–22.

16. Tocqueville, 301–19.

17. Laurence Sterne, *The Life and Opinions of Tristram Shandy, Gentleman*, Modern Library ed. (New York: Modern Library, 2004). Hereafter referred to as *Tristram Shandy*.

18. Sterne, *Tristram Shandy, Gentleman*, 2.12.

19. The term "hobby-horse" has an interesting history. Sterne, no doubt, is aware of its usage in Shakespeare as a term for a prostitute. See William Shakespeare, *Othello*, 3rd ed., ed. E. A. J. Honigmann (New York: Arden Shakespeare, 1996), 4.1.

20. Sterne, *Tristram Shandy*, 1.7.

21. Tocqueville, *Democracy in America*, 2.1.9.

22. Tocqueville, 2.1.17.

23. Tocqueville, 2.1.9.
24. Tocqueville, 60.

Conclusion

1. Kathryn Hymes, "'The Great Resignation' Misses the Point," *Wired*, November 1, 2021, https://www.wired.com/story/great-resignation-misses-the-point/.

2. Cal Newport, "Why Are So Many Knowledge Workers Quitting?," *New Yorker*, August 16, 2021, https://www.newyorker.com/culture/office-space/why-are-so-many-knowledge-workers-quitting.

3. Derek Thompson, "Three Myths of the Great Resignation," *The Atlantic*, December 8, 2021, https://www.theatlantic.com/ideas/archive/2021/12/great-resignation-myths-quitting-jobs/620927/.

Bibliography

Ackerman, Bruce. *Social Justice in the Liberal State*. New Haven, CT: Yale University Press, 1980.

Adorno, Theodor W. *The Culture Industry: Selected Essays on Mass Culture*. Edited by J. M. Bernstein. New York: Routledge, 1991.

Arendt, Hannah. *The Human Condition*. Garden City: Anchor Books, 1959.

Aristotle. *Aristotle: Selections*. Translated by Terence Irwin and Gail Fine. Indianapolis: Hackett, 1995.

———. *Aristotle's "Metaphysics."* Translated by J. Sachs. Santa Fe, NM: Green Lion Press, 1999.

———. *Aristotle's "Nicomachean Ethics."* Translated by Robert C. Bartlett and Susan D. Collins. Chicago: University of Chicago Press, 2012.

———. *Aristotle's "Nicomachean Ethics."* Translated by J. Sachs. Newbury, MA: Focus, 2002.

———. *Aristotle's "Politics": Second Edition*. Translated by C. Lord. Chicago: University of Chicago Press, 2013.

———. *Politics: Books VII and VIII*. Translated by R. Kraut. Oxford: Clarendon Press, 1998.

Baltes, John. "Locke's Inverted Quarantine: Discipline, Panopticism, and the Making of the Liberal Subject." *Review of Politics* 75, no. 2 (2013): 173–92.

Barry, Brian. *The Liberal Theory of Justice*. Oxford: Oxford University Press, 1973.

Bartlett, Robert C. "The 'Realism' of Classical Political Science." *American Journal of Political Science* 38, no. 2 (1994): 381–402.

Bartlett, Robert, and Mary Nichols. "Aristotle's Science of the Best Regime." *American Political Science Review* 89 (1995): 152–60.

Baumann, Zygmunt. *Work, Consumerism and the New Poor*. Buckingham: Open University Press, 1998.

Berkowitz, Peter. *Virtue and the Making of Modern Liberalism*, 2nd ed. Princeton, NJ: Princeton University Press, 1999.

Berry, Wendell. *Hannah Coulter*. Berkeley, CA: Counterpoint Press, 2005.

138 | Bibliography

Black, Jeff J. S. *Rousseau's Critique of Science: A Commentary on the Discourse on the Sciences and the Arts*. Lanham, MD: Lexington Books, 2009.

Brubaker, Stanley C. "Coming into One's Own: John Locke's Theory of Property, God, and Politics." *Review of Politics* 74, no. 2 (2012): 207–32.

Butterworth, Charles E. "Interpretive Essay." In *The Reveries of the Solitary Walker*, 145–240. Indianapolis: Hackett, 1992.

Cantor, Paul. "The Metaphysics of Botany: Rousseau and the New Criticism of Plants." *Southwest Review* 70, no. 3 (1985): 362–80.

Carrig, Joseph. "Liberal Impediments to Liberal Education: The Assent to Locke." *Review of Politics* 63, no. 1 (2001): 41–76.

Casson, Douglas. *Liberating Judgment: Fanatics, Skeptics, and John Locke's Politics of Probability*. Princeton, NJ: Princeton University Press, 2011.

Collins, Susan D. *Aristotle and the Rediscovery of Citizenship*. New York: Cambridge University Press, 2009.

Cooper, Laurence D. *Eros in Plato, Rousseau, and Nietzsche: The Politics of Infinity*. University Park: Pennsylvania State University Press, 2008.

———. *Rousseau, Nature, and the Problem of the Good Life*. University Park: Pennsylvania State University Press, 1999.

Davis, Michael. *The Autobiography of Philosophy*. Lanham, MD: Rowman & Littlefield, 1999.

Dawson, Jane. "A History of Vocation: Tracing a Keyword of Work, Meaning, and Moral Purpose." *Adult Education Quarterly* 55, no. 3 (2005): 220–31.

de Botton, Alain. *The Pleasures and Sorrows of Work*. New York: Vintage, 2010.

de Grazia, Sebastian. *Of Time, Work, and Leisure*. Millwood, NY: Kraus International, 1962.

Depew, David J. "Politics, Music, and Contemplation in Aristotle's Ideal State." In *A Companion to Aristotle's Politics*, edited by David Keyt and Fred D. Miller Jr., 346–80. Oxford: Blackwell, 1991.

Derrida, Jacques. *Of Grammatology*. Translated by Gayatri Chakravorty Spivak. Baltimore: Johns Hopkins University Press, 2016.

Destrée, Pierre. "Education, Leisure, and Politics." In *The Cambridge Companion to Aristotle's "Politics,"* edited by M. Deslauriers and P. Destrée, 301–23. Cambridge: Cambridge University Press, 2013.

Dienstag, Joshua Foa. "Serving God and Mammon: The Lockean Sympathy in Early American Political Thought." *American Political Science Review* 90, no. 3 (1996): 497–511. https://doi.org/10.2307/2082605.

Douglass, Frederick. "A Friendly Word to Maryland." In *The Frederick Douglass Papers: Volume 4, Series One: Speeches, Debates, and Interviews, 1864-80*, edited by John W. Blassingame and John R. McKivigan IV, 38–50. New Haven, CT: Yale University Press, 1991.

———. *Narrative of the Life of Frederick Douglass*. Mineola, NY: Dover, 1995.

———. "Third Annual Fair of the Tennessee Colored Agricultural and Mechanical Association." Nashville, TN, September 18, 1873.

Dunn, John. *The Political Thought of John Locke: An Historical Account of the Argument of the "Two Treatises of Government."* Cambridge: Cambridge University Press, 1982.

Fustel de Coulanges, N. D. *The Ancient City: A Study of the Religion, Laws, and Institutions of Greece and Rome.* Translated by W. Small. Mineola, NY: Dover, 2006.

Galston, William A. *Liberal Purposes: Goods, Virtues, and Diversity in the Liberal State.* New York: Cambridge University Press, 1991.

Gauthier, David. *Rousseau: The Sentiment of Existence.* Cambridge: Cambridge University Press, 2006.

Goldman, Harvey. *Max Weber and Thomas Mann: Calling and the Shaping of the Self.* Berkeley: University of California Press, 1988.

Goodman, Dena. *The Republic of Letters: A Cultural History of the French Enlightenment.* Ithaca, NY: Cornell University Press, 1994.

Gourevitch, Victor. "A Provisional Reading of Rousseau's 'Reveries of the Solitary Walker.'" *Review of Politics* 74, no. 3 (2012): 489–518.

Grace, Eve. "The Restlessness of 'Being': Rousseau's Protean Sentiment of Existence." *History of European Ideas* 27, no. 2 (January 1, 2001): 133–51.

Grant, Ruth W. *Hypocrisy and Integrity: Machiavelli, Rousseau, and the Ethics of Politics.* Chicago: University of Chicago Press, 1997.

Huizinga, Johan. *Homo Ludens: A Study of the Play-Element in Culture.* Boston, MA: Beacon Press, 1955.

Hulliung, Mark. *The Autocritique of Enlightenment: Rousseau and the Philosophes.* Cambridge, MA: Harvard University Press, 1994.

Hundert, E. J. "The Making of Homo Faber: John Locke between Ideology and History." *Journal of the History of Ideas* 33, no. 1 (1972): 3–22.

Hymes, Kathryn. "'The Great Resignation' Misses the Point." *Wired*, November 1, 2021. https://www.wired.com/story/great-resignation-misses-the-point/.

Kautz, Steven. *Liberalism and Community.* Ithaca, NY: Cornell University Press, 1997.

Kelly, Christopher. "Rousseau and the Case against (and for) the Arts." In *The Legacy of Rousseau,* edited by Clifford Orwin and Nathan Tarcov, 20–44. Chicago: University of Chicago Press, 1997.

———. *Rousseau's Exemplary Life: The "Confessions" as Political Philosophy.* Ithaca, NY: Cornell University Press, 1987.

King, Peter. *The Life and Letters of John Locke: With Extracts from His Journals and Commonplace Books.* London: John Childs and Son, 1858.

Kingwell, Mark. *Catch and Release: Trout Fishing and the Meaning of Life.* New York: Penguin Books, 2004.

140 | Bibliography

———. *Measure Yourself against the Earth*. Windsor, ON: Biblioasis, 2015.

Koganzon, Rita. " 'Contesting the Empire of Habit': Habituation and Liberty in Lockean Education." *American Political Science Review* 110, no. 3 (August 2016): 547–58.

Krantz-Kent, Rachel. "Television, Capturing America's Attention at Prime Time and Beyond." *Beyond the Numbers* 7, no. 14 (September 2018). https://www.bls.gov/opub/btn/volume-7/television-capturing-americas-attention.htm.

Kraut, Richard. *Aristotle on the Human Good*. Princeton, NJ: Princeton University Press, 1989.

———. *Aristotle: Political Philosophy*. Oxford: Oxford University Press, 2002.

Lamprecht, Sterling. *The Moral and Political Philosophy of John Locke*. New York: Columbia University Press, 1918.

Lane, Joseph H. "Reverie and the Return to Nature: Rousseau's Experience of Convergence." *Review of Politics* 68, no. 3 (2006): 474–99.

Lasch, Christopher. *The Culture of Narcissism: American Life in an Age of Diminishing Expectations*. New York: W. W. Norton, 1991.

Lepper, Mark R., David Greene, and Richard E. Nisbett. "Undermining Children's Intrinsic Interest with Extrinsic Reward: A Test of the 'Overjustification' Hypothesis." *Journal of Personality and Social Psychology* 28, no. 1 (1973): 129–37.

Locke, John. *An Essay Concerning Human Understanding*. Edited by Peter H. Nidditch. Oxford: Oxford University Press, 1979.

———. "First Treatise." In *Locke: Two Treatises of Government*, 3rd ed., edited by Peter Laslett, 141–264. Cambridge: Cambridge University Press, 1988.

———. "Of the Conduct of the Understanding." In *Some Thoughts Concerning Education and Of the Conduct of the Understanding*, edited by Ruth Weissbourd Grant and Nathan Tarcov, 163–227. Indianapolis: Hackett, 1996.

———. "Second Treatise." In *Locke: Two Treatises of Government*, 3rd ed., edited by Peter Laslett, 265–428. Cambridge England ; New York: Cambridge University Press, 1988.

———. "Some Thoughts Concerning Education." In *Some Thoughts Concerning Education and Of the Conduct of the Understanding*, edited by Ruth W. Grant and Nathan Tarcov, 1–162. Indianapolis: Hackett, 1996.

Lord, Carnes. *Education and Culture in the Political Thought of Aristotle*. Ithaca, NY: Cornell University Press, 1982.

Macedo, Stephen. *Liberal Virtues: Citizenship, Virtue, and Community in Liberal Constitutionalism*. Oxford: Clarendon Press, 1990.

Maclean, Norman. *A River Runs Through It and Other Stories*. Chicago: University of Chicago Press, 2001.

Macpherson, C. B. *The Political Theory of Possessive Individualism: Hobbes to Locke*. Don Mills, ON: Oxford University Press, 2011.

Bibliography | 141

Manent, Pierre. *An Intellectual History of Liberalism*. Translated by Rebecca Balinski. Princeton, NJ: Princeton University Press, 1996.

———. *Tocqueville and the Nature of Democracy*. Translated by John Waggoner. Lanham, MD: Rowman & Littlefield, 1996.

Marks, Jonathan. *Perfection and Disharmony in the Thought of Jean-Jacques Rousseau*. Cambridge: Cambridge University Press, 2005.

———. "Who Lost Nature? Rousseau and Rousseauism." *Polity* 34, no. 4 (June 1, 2002): 479–502.

Marshall, John S. "Aristotle and the Agrarians." *Review of Politics* 9 (1947): 350–61.

Marshall, Paul. "John Locke: Between God and Mammon." *Canadian Journal of Political Science* 12, no. 1 (1979): 73–96.

Martela, Frank, and Anne B. Pessi. "Significant Work Is about Self-Realization and Broader Purpose: Defining the Key Dimensions of Meaningful Work." *Frontiers in Psychology* 9 (2018). https://doi.org/10.3389/fpsyg.2018.00363.

Martin, Waldo E., Jr. *The Mind of Frederick Douglass*. Chapel Hill: University of North Carolina Press, 1984.

Masters, Roger D. *The Political Philosophy of Rousseau*. Princeton, NJ: Princeton University Press, 1968.

McGuane, Thomas. *The Longest Silence: A Life in Fishing*. New York: Vintage, 1999.

McLendon, Michael Locke. "Rousseau, Amour Propre, and Intellectual Celebrity." *Journal of Politics* 71, no. 2 (2009): 506–19.

Mehta, Uday Singh. *The Anxiety of Freedom: Imagination and Individuality in Locke's Political Thought*. Ithaca, NY: Cornell University Press, 1992.

Meier, Heinrich. *On the Happiness of the Philosophic Life: Reflections on Rousseau's Rêveries in Two Books*. Translated by Robert Berman. Chicago: University of Chicago Press, 2016.

Melzer, Arthur M. *The Natural Goodness of Man: On the System of Rousseau's Thought*. Chicago: University of Chicago Press, 1990.

Mendham, Matthew D. "Gentle Savages and Fierce Citizens against Civilization: Unraveling Rousseau's Paradoxes." *American Journal of Political Science* 55, no. 1 (2011): 170–87.

———. "Rebuking the Enlightenment Establishments, Bourgeois and Aristocratic: Rousseau's Ambivalence about Leisure." In *The Palgrave Handbook of Leisure Theory*, edited by Karl Spracklen, Brett Lashua, Erin Sharpe, and Spencer Swain, 271–88. London: Palgrave Macmillan, 2017.

Mumby, Dennis K. "Work: What Is It Good For? (Absolutely Nothing)—a Critical Theorist's Perspective." *Industrial and Organizational Psychology* 12, no. 4 (2019): 429–43.

Myers, Peter C. *Frederick Douglass: Race and the Rebirth of American Liberalism*. Lawrence: University Press of Kansas, 2008.

———. *Our Only Star and Compass*. Lanham, MD: Rowman & Littlefield, 1999.

142 | Bibliography

Nazar, Hina. "Locke, Education, and 'Disciplinary Liberalism.'" *Review of Politics* 79, no. 2 (2017): 215–38.

Neal, Patrick. "Vulgar Liberalism." *Political Theory* 21, no. 4 (1993): 623–42.

Newport, Cal. "Why Are So Many Knowledge Workers Quitting?" *New Yorker*, August 16, 2021. https://www.newyorker.com/culture/office-space/why-are-so-many-knowledge-workers-quitting.

Nussbaum, Martha. *The Fragility of Goodness: Luck and Ethics in Greek Tragedy and Philosophy*. Cambridge: Cambridge University Press, 1986.

Ortega y Gasset, Jose. *Meditations on Hunting*. Translated by Howard B. Wescott. New York: Charles Scribner's Sons, 1986.

Owens, Joseph. "Aristotle on Leisure." *Canadian Journal of Philosophy* 11 (1981): 713–23.

Palmer, Parker J. *Let Your Life Speak: Listening for the Voice of Vocation*. San Francisco: Jossey-Bass, 2000.

Pangle, Thomas L. *The Spirit of Modern Republicanism: The Moral Vision of the American Founders and the Philosophy of Locke*. Chicago: University of Chicago Press, 1988.

Paulsen, Roland. *Empty Labor: Idleness and Workplace Resistance*. Cambridge: Cambridge University Press, 2014.

Pieper, Josef. *Leisure: The Basis of Culture*. Translated by G. Marsbary. South Bend, IN: St. Augustine's Press, 1998.

Pittz, Steven F. "Identity and the Practice of American Citizenship: From Transcendentalists to Identitarians." In *American Citizenship and Constitutionalism in Principle and Practice*, edited by Steven F. Pittz and Joseph Postell, 56–82. Norman: University of Oklahoma Press, 2022.

Plutarch. *Plutarch's Lives Volume 1*. Edited by A. H. Clough, translated by J. Dryden. New York: Modern Library, 2001.

Rapaczynski, Andrzej. "Locke's Conception of Property and the Principle of Sufficient Reason." *Journal of the History of Ideas* 42, no. 2 (1981): 305–15.

Rawls, John. *Political Liberalism*. Expanded ed. New York: Columbia University Press, 2005.

Rose, Julie. *Free Time*. Princeton, NJ: Princeton University Press, 2016.

Rousseau, Jean-Jacques. *Emile: Or On Education*. Edited by Christopher Kelly. Translated by Allan Bloom. Hanover, NH: Dartmouth College Press, 2009.

———. "Essay on the Origin of Languages." In *The First and Second Discourses and Essay on the Origin of Languages*, translated by Victor Gourevitch, 239–95. New York: Harper & Row, 1986.

———. *The First and Second Discourses*. Edited by Roger D. Masters. Translated by Roger D. Masters and Judith R. Masters. New York: St. Martin's Press, 1964.

———. "Last Reply." In *The First and Second Discourses and Essay on the Origin of Languages*, 65–89. New York: Harper & Row, 1986.

Bibliography | 143

———. *Letter to D'Alembert and Writings for the Theater*. Edited by Christopher Kelly and Allan Bloom. Translated by Allan Bloom. Hanover, NH: University Press of New England, 2004.

———. "Letters to Malesherbes." In *The Confessions: And Correspondence, Including the Letters to Malesherbes*, edited by Christopher Kelly, Roger D. Masters, and Peter G. Stillman, translated by Christopher Kelly, 572–83. The Collected Writings of Rousseau 5. Hanover, NH: University Press of New England, 1995.

———. *The Plan for Perpetual Peace, On the Government of Poland, and Other Writings on History and Politics*. Hanover: Dartmouth College Press, 2011.

———. *The Reveries of the Solitary Walker*. Translated by Charles E. Butterworth. Indianapolis: Hackett, 1992.

Ryan, Alan. *Property and Political Theory*. New York: Blackwell, 1984.

———. "The Romantic Theory of Ownership." In *The Making of Modern Liberalism*, 586–99. Princeton, NJ: Princeton University Press, 2012.

Saint-Amand, Pierre. *The Pursuit of Laziness: An Idle Interpretation of the Enlightenment*. Princeton, NJ: Princeton University Press, 2011.

Salkever, Stephen G. "Rousseau & the Concept of Happiness." *Polity* 11, no. 1 (1978): 27–45.

———. "Whose Prayer? The Best Regime of Book 7 and the Lessons of Aristotle's 'Politics.'" *Political Theory* 35 (2007): 29–46.

Satkunanandan, Shalini. "Max Weber and the Ethos of Politics beyond Calculation." *American Political Science Review* 108, no. 1 (2014): 169–81.

Schwartz, Joel. *The Sexual Politics of Jean-Jacques Rousseau*. Chicago: University of Chicago Press, 1984.

Shakespeare, William. *Othello*, 3rd ed. Edited by E. A. J. Honigmann. New York: Arden Shakespeare, 1996.

Shklar, Judith N. *American Citizenship: The Quest for Inclusion*. Cambridge, MA: Harvard University Press, 1998.

———. *Men and Citizens: A Study of Rousseau's Social Theory*. London: Cambridge University Press, 1985.

Smith, Rogers M. *Liberalism and American Constitutional Law*. Cambridge, MA: Harvard University Press, 1985.

Solmsen, Friedrich. "Leisure and Play in Aristotle's Ideal State." *Rheinisches Museum Für Philologie* 107 (1964): 193–220.

Starobinski, Jean. *Jean-Jacques Rousseau: Transparency and Obstruction*. Translated by Arthur Goldhammer. Chicago: University of Chicago Press, 1988.

Starr, Bradley E. "The Structure of Max Weber's Ethic of Responsibility." *Journal of Religious Ethics* 27, no. 3 (1999): 407–34.

Sterne, Laurence. *The Life and Opinions of Tristram Shandy, Gentleman*. Modern Library ed. New York: Modern Library, 2004.

144 | Bibliography

Stocks, J. L. "ΣΧΟΛΗ." *Classical Quarterly* 30 (1936): 177–87.

Storey, Benjamin. "Rousseau and the Problem of Self-Knowledge." *Review of Politics* 71, no. 2 (2009): 251–74.

Strauss, Leo. *The City and Man*. Chicago: University of Chicago Press, 1978.

———. *Natural Right and History*. Chicago: University of Chicago Press, 1953.

———. *Natural Right and History*. Revised ed. Chicago: University of Chicago Press, 1999.

———. "On the Intention of Rousseau." *Social Research* 14, no. 1 (1947): 455–87.

Supiano, Beckie. "How Liberal-Arts Majors Fare over the Long Haul." *Chronicle of Higher Education*, January 22, 2014. https://www.chronicle.com/article/How-Liberal-Arts-Majors-Fare/144133.

Swanson, Judith A. *The Public and the Private in Aristotle's Political Philosophy*. Ithaca, NY: Cornell University Press, 1992.

Sylvester, Charles. "The Classical Idea of Leisure: Cultural Ideal or Class Prejudice?" *Leisure Sciences* 21, no. 1 (1999): 3–16.

Tarcov, Nathan. *Locke's Education for Liberty*. Chicago: University of Chicago Press, 1989.

Taylor, Charles. *Sources of the Self: The Making of the Modern Identity*. Cambridge: Cambridge University Press, 1989.

Tessitore, Aristide. "Making the City Safe for Philosophy: *Nicomachean Ethics*, Book 10." *American Political Science Review* 84 (1990): 1256–57.

Thompson, Derek. "Three Myths of the Great Resignation." *The Atlantic*, December 8, 2021. https://www.theatlantic.com/ideas/archive/2021/12/great-resignation-myths-quitting-jobs/620927/.

Tocqueville, Alexis de. *Democracy in America*. Translated by Arthur Goldhammer. New York: Library of America, 2004.

Todorov, Tzvetan. *Frail Happiness*. Translated by John T. Scott and Robert D. Zaretsky. University Park: Penn State University Press, 2001.

Tomasi, John. *Liberalism beyond Justice: Citizens, Society, and the Boundaries of Political Theory*. Princeton, NJ: Princeton University Press, 2021.

Turner, Stephen. Introduction to *The Cambridge Companion to Weber*, 1–18. Cambridge: Cambridge University Press, 2000.

Vander Waerdt, P. A. "Kingship and Philosophy in Aristotle's Best Regime." *Phronesis* 30 (1985): 249–73.

Waldron, Jeremy. *The Right to Private Property*. Oxford: Clarendon Press, 1991.

Weber, Marianne. *Max Weber: Ein Lebensbild*. Tübingen: Mohr Siebeck, 1984.

Weber, Max. *The Protestant Ethic and the Spirit of Capitalism: And Other Writings*. Edited by Peter Baehr and Gordon C. Wells. New York: Penguin Classics, 2002.

———. *The Vocation Lectures*. Edited by David Owen and Tracy B. Strong. Translated by Rodney Livingstone. Indianapolis: Hackett, 2004.

Wood, Neal. *The Politics of Locke's Philosophy: A Social Study of an Essay Concerning Human Understanding.* Berkeley: University of California Press, 1983.

Yack, Bernard. *The Problems of a Political Animal: Community, Justice, and Conflict in Aristotelian Political Thought.* Berkeley: University of California Press, 1993.

Zuckert, Catherine. "Aristotle on the Limits and Satisfactions of Political Life." *Interpretation* 11 (1983): 202.

Zuckert, Michael P. *The Natural Rights Republic: Studies in the Foundation of the American Political Tradition.* Notre Dame, IN: University of Notre Dame Press, 1997.

Index

Arendt, Hannah, 3
aristocracy, 27, 29, 38–42, 60–61, 66, 84, 105–106, 115, 128n54
Aristotle, 3–5, 7, 11–28, 114–16; on courage, 18, 24; on education, 11, 16–17, 23, 26–27, 63, 106; on *energeia*, 15, 24, 28; on the ideal regime, 4, 13, 15, 17, 22–25, 69, 114–15; on inequality, 4, 12, 87; on intellectual virtue, 4, 12–15, 17, 20, 53, 74–75, 114; on moderation, 17–21, 24, 108; on moral virtue, 4, 13, 20–21, 26–28, 120n18; on music, 25–28, 93, 97, 106; on philosophy, 20–21, 27; on play, 11, 23–26, 92, 94, 97, 105; on the political life, 22–25; on Sparta, 15, 18–21, 60, 120n1; on work, 27, 51, 60
automation, 4, 11–12

beauty, 26–28, 94–99, 106–107
Berry, Wendell, 64

Cantor, Paul, 77, 86
capitalism, 50, 63–64, 96, 99–100, 109

de Botton, Alain, 49, 65
democracy, 2, 5, 11, 40, 51, 61, 92, 101–102, 106–108, 113–115

Douglass, Frederick, 42–47
Dunn, John, 38

egalitarianism. *See* equality
equality, 7, 22, 29, 31, 41–42, 102, 106–107, 114–15

fishing, 93–100, 105–107, 114
freedom, 3, 6–7, 12, 14, 23–24, 29, 31, 34, 42–46, 50, 60, 66–67, 69–70, 75, 81, 87–89, 102, 114, 119n1

Galston, William A., 35
Great Resignation, 1, 112–113

hedonism, 33
hobbies, 7–8, 92–108

intellectual history, 2–3, 114

Kingwell, Mark, 98

laziness, 36, 42, 47, 73, 78, 81–82
liberalism, 28–32, 46, 49, 68, 100, 106, 109
Locke, John, 5–6, 29–48; on the calling, 38, 41; on education, 38–39; on industriousness 5–6, 31, 36, 41–42; on innate ideas, 34–35; on pleasure and pain, 30–34, 37–42;

148 | Index

Locke, John *(continued)*
on property, 5, 30–33, 42; on
reason, 33–37, 44; on recreation, 5,
38–41, 100

Maclean, Norman, 96, 98
Manent, Pierre, 101, 122n6
Marks, Jonathan, 72
Marx, Karl, 30, 32, 63, 99–100
McGuane, Thomas, 95–96, 134n6
Meier, Heinrich, 82–83
Melzer, Arthur, 83

Palmer, Parker, 66–67
Pieper, Josef, 11, 25
poetry, 105–107
Protestantism, 50, 57–59, 61

Quiet Quitting, 1, 111, 113

revolution, 3, 69–70, 96
rights, 1, 8–9, 29, 33, 43, 45–49, 93,
111
Rose, Julie, 8
Rousseau, Jean-Jacques, 6–7, 69–90,
114–117; on botany, 75–79, 85–86;
on the citizen, 70, 72, 80, 83–87;
on civilization, 70–73, 76–77; on
duty, 6–7, 70, 73–74, 76–78, 81,
88–89; on the expansion of being,
79–83; on foresight, 76–79, 81; on
freedom, 69–70, 75, 81, 87–89; on
imagination, 82–83; on laziness,

73, 78, 81–82; on luxury, 86; on
moral defense of idleness, 83–86;
on reason, 74–79; on sentiment of
existence, 71–72, 74–75, 77–78, 81;
on solitude, 71–74, 78, 85–87; on
vanity, 70, 73, 78, 84–89, 104,
116
Ryan, Alan, 30–32

Sabbath, 102
Saint-Armand, Pierre, 77, 79–80, 85
self-control, 33–34, 37, 50–51, 57–58,
63
slavery, 4, 42–44, 47, 69
Sterne, Laurence, 103–104
Strauss, Leo, 32, 62

Taylor, Charles, 35
technology, 1, 3–4, 111–112
television, 92–93, 101, 105, 109
Tocqueville, Alexis de, 11, 51,
101–102, 105–109
Todorov, Tzvetan, 82
toleration, 30, 107

vocation, 5–7, 49–68, 91–92, 102–104,
108, 113, 115

Waldron, Jeremy, 30–32
Weber, Max, 6, 50–68; on personality,
56–58; on politics as a vocation,
50–56; on science as a vocation,
52–53, 56, 58; on vanity 54–56, 67